First Tango In Warsaw

Poland 1926
Short lived togetherness with parents and my elder brother Rafal.

Wanda Blocka
Warschau Celesnikaş

8 DEUTSCHES REICH GENERALGOUVERNEMENT
10 DEUTSCHES REICH GENERALGOUVERNEMENT
12 GENERALGOUVERNEMENT

Herrn

Zavalski Leon

Sprawdzono
w Kartotece
P.C.K.

Lisboa - Portugal
R. Alexandre Herculano 41 r/c

Sprawdzono

5185

Warschau 3. IX. 1943.

Liebesgabe, zwei Schachtel Sardinien
habe ich erhalten. Vielen Dank dafür.

mit herzlichsten Grüßen

Wanda Blocka

784050 peul
Blocka J.   Ggk Podchoro
11980

First Tango In Warsaw

Memories of a
Polish Pilot in World War 2

Jack Blocki

A SQUARE ONE PUBLICATION

First published in 1997 by
Square One Publications,
The Tudor House
Upton upon Severn, Worcs. WR8 0HT

British Cataloguing Data is available for this title

ISBN 1 899955 27 5

Typeset in Times New Roman 11 on 13 by Avon Dataset Ltd,
Bidford-on-Avon, Warwickshire, B50 4JH

Printed by CPI Antony Rowe, Chippenham, Wiltshire

To all my comrades in Bomber Command
who sacrificed so much for so little.

Foreword

Without doubt the Royal Air Force Bomber Command played a unique and crucial role in bringing the industrial might of the Third Reich to its knees in World War II. Over 125,000 Service personnel from many Allied nations served in the Command, of which some 60% sustained injuries of one form or another. Jacek (Jack) Blocki was one of these Servicemen who managed to avoid becoming a casualty, and went on to complete 37 years in the Royal Air Force. Having managed to flee his native Poland, Jack found himself on HMS Arandora Star which reached England in 1940. By the summer of that year he had completed basic flying training and moved onto Wellingtons. Thereafter, Jack takes us through his career which saw him complete 2 tours on Bombers and come out relatively unscathed – a feat which was achieved by only 65 other aircrew – and onto Cyprus where he and his wife decided to settle together with 'Smoocher' – an ocean going sloop – in 1973. However, danger was not too far away in the form of the Turkish/ Greek confrontation in 1974 and, once again, Jack was in the centre of the hostilities as an emergency controller at Nicosia airport.

Jack offers, in this book, a lively personal account of the part he played in the Bomber Command campaign, and highlights the important contribution of the Polish aircrew contingent. Such personal recollections add an important depth to our understanding of wartime campaigns. The book reveals sympathetically the immediate and close bond of the aircrew, and how that spirit continued throughout the War. His personal description and anecdotes provide a genuine account of real aircrew activity during the War, together with his subsequent experiences in Malaya and Cyprus. This story adds a valuable insight into large and small scale conflict and the personal price all involved must bear.

P MILLAR, Air Vice-Marshal
Commander, British Forces Cyprus

Contents

*Post matriculation holiday
with class pals – 1939*

CHAPTER I

Beginning Of The End

The official reception in the Bomber Command Headquarters is about to reveal its secret. Large dining room tables had been cleared, except for silver and crystal decanters, and the last waiter closes the doors behind him. Even after two glasses of wine I find my youthful appearance here in the uniform of a Flying Officer slightly embarassing and out of place despite the fatherly, though rather patronising attentions of a Colonel on one side and a Group Captain on the other. Across the table to my right, dinner jackets and grey suits intermingle with high ranking badges of the Royal Air Force. Suddenly, a loud rap of a gavel silences the smoke filled room.

'Distinguished Guests, Gentlemen. Please pay attention to the British Foreign Minister, the Right Honorable Anthony Eden.' The tall, meticulously elegant figure of Churchill's right hand man rises from the chair. All eyes focus in his direction.

'Tonight I would like to present to you the new Polish Prime Minister, Mr Arciszewski and his Cabinet, most of whom arrived in London very recently from their war torn country courtesy of a daring plan and our brave airmen.' To a burst of applause he points to a group of civilian guests. I stare between the two candelabras on my table at the faces which seem vaguely familiar. Faces no longer distorted by the anxiety I saw in the moonlight as I bundled them into my aircraft while the firing commenced around the strip, vigorously defended by the Polish underground army. So, these are the people I extracted from under the noses of the German and Russian armies only two weeks ago!

The speech continues: 'These gentlemen had been at the heart of

1

the resistance against the Nazi oppressors throughout the occupation of Poland and their presence here in London at this time should revitalise the hopes of this courageous, long suffering nation. The only occupied nation which has not added a single Quisling to the infamous list of Hitler's collaborators . . .'

I feel proud and hardly hear the praises for all involved including myself which conclude the introductions. Six hours later, still trying to digest the excitement of last night's events, I am in a coach heading for Euston station and the next train home. There is something familiar about the bomb scarred city with ruined buildings on every street and a packed railway station full of anxious looking passengers. I am told that a German rocket smashed into the railway yards only minutes before my arrival and all departures are indefinitely postponed. Nothing to do but wait . . . After queueing for what seemed like ages I manage to cheer myself up with a cup of tea and succeed in finding a seat in the crowded waiting room. Through the mist of memories a similar situation of not so long ago reappears like the ghosts of a distant past and I find myself waiting for another train on another station far away. Half asleep I can hear the distant whistle of the steam engine approaching, then, a shrill, distorted voice of a female station announcer brings me instantly back to reality: 'The train arriving on platform 6 is the 8 o'clock Glasgow express stopping at Crewe, Preston and . . .'

I ignore the rest of the announcement, grab my bag and run through the crowd and over the bridge to platform 6. I am lucky to find a seat in a first class compartment which within minutes is bulging with passengers and their luggage. I look at my watch. It is midday. An army Captain next to me apologises for the squeeze. His elbow is pressing on my ribs but I tell him not to worry. As the train finally moves slowly out of Euston station everyone in the compartment settles for a long journey, still polite and apparently, well used to the discomforts of wartime travel. Once again the uncanny similarity of this morning's events takes me back to those momentous days which had dictated my life ever since. I close my eyes. Yes, now I remember the date even and I let the nonchalantly erased past return to the beginning of it all.

The dawn of 13th September 1939 heralded another fine day with not a cloud in the sky. Not that myself, my brother Rafal or the rest of the sufferers on our packed train cared about the weather. During the past two nights each stop had become a boring routine. I opened my eyes and vainly attempted to stretch stiff limbs locked between two bodies and a wooden bench which used to be 3rd class seat for four passengers but now accommodated seven. Across, Rafal was still asleep, glasses down his nose, his head against the window supported by a satchel which served us well since mother packed it so caringly on that fateful day in Warsaw. Acrid smell of the burning city still in my nostrils, I could see her again in the fading light of the Central Station, tears streaming unashamedly down her face as she tried to rise above the bustling crowd of would be passengers for the last glimpse of her sons. I struggled to the window just as the overloaded train shuddered and screeched noisily forward: 'Don't worry Mamusia,' I yelled as hard as I could: 'We shall soon be back . . . after we beat hell out of the Hun!' Soon, in total darkness, we settled to the rhythmic wheel clatter and regained some of our youthful over-confidence. Although not yet in uniform we were only too ready to fight the invaders, hoping to reinforce our retreating armies which, according to plan, were to form second line of defence along river Bug. 'No, we are not the boys to give in, blitzkrieg or no blitzkrieg! The might of our western Allies will soon send Hitler and his gang packing and that is only a matter of time.' This type of conversation may have been good for the morale but, of course, had nothing to do with reality. Previous days after sudden German attacks, especially from the air, had little effect on my patriotic indoctrination or loyalty to the cause. Like all the students caught in the middle of school holidays I was issued with a large spade and enthusiastically dug zigzag trenches around Mokotow Airport and surrounding installations while unmolested Stuka bombers blasted everything in sight. Occasional panic did not last long, after all we had to win this war! I might even make that course in architecture in Poznan university in few weeks time, I thought. How proud was my father when he received the news of acceptance after better than expected matriculation results. At seventeen, I was told, I did exceptionally well in projected geometry apart from advanced level mathematics, subjects of some mystery in pre-computer days. Family joy, however, lasted only few days as father was back in his Colonel's uniform, recalled to active service at a short notice, destination unknown, swept on the rapidly rising tide of chaotic war preparations.

Any thoughts which flashed through my mind during the cramped awakening to the sound of desynchronised breathing of men and an atmosphere one could cut with a knife vaporised instantly with loud-mouthed bellowing down the corridor: 'EVERYBODY OUT! EVERYBODY OUT! Get your kit and outside, szybko, szybko!' In the scramble that followed it is a wonder no one was crushed or suffocated. Jumping off the high mounted carriages was equally asking for an injury. I found myself in a cornfield filling my lungs with long overdue fresh air of the countryside. Agitated people were still streaming out of the train looking up apprehensibly and waiting, no doubt, for sound of aeroplanes. Trampling through chest high corn I found Rafal at last. 'Look at that locomotive, it's had it,' he pointed to the big black monster ahead of abandoned carriages, motionless and obviously unable to puff either through lack of coal or water, 'Zbych and Voytek have gone there to find out where we are.' He wiped his glasses on the sleeve. 'Look at this lot, they are already drifting away . . . and who can blame them . . . this train is asking to be hit.'

I began to feel rather edgy. 'So what on earth are we doing here in the open,' I asked.

'Let's go!'

'Hold on Jacek, (In Polish J=Y and C=TS, it's easy!) not so fast, without these two we have no chance.'

'And what if they don't come back?'

My feeble question did not get a reply and I did not persist knowing down deep that he was right. Our two train companions did not come from the world of city apartments, clean sheets, doting parents, higher or any education but their tales of life and survival on the Warsaw streets sounded impressive to my naive mind. Equally, I felt, they were quietly anxious to hear from the horse's mouth how the other half lived. It was noticeable also that our short lived acquaintance gained importance during a long stop in Lublin station when Rafal produced some cash and paid for the refreshments.

With so many heads poking out of the corn and moving in all directions we did not notice their return until unmistakable Varsovian voice came through from nearby: 'Come on, come on, are you two waiting for applause . . . ?' Our instant mates represented a youthful pair, Zbych tall and slim, straw-blond hair hanging untidily beneath a worn flat cap, which also gave shelter to a most inquiring and alert pair of blue eyes, while Voytek, built like a tank, could have easily performed as a wrestler under the name of Teenage Giant Mauler if it was not for his pinky face of a cherub.

'The news,' says Zbych, 'is not very clever, we are somewhere near Yaroslav, wherever that is in this prairie,' he waved his hand in disgust as he took deep breath . . . 'Some fellows heard on the radio that Warsaw is completely surrounded but fighting goes on, the bastards! Our best bet, I reckon, is to leave this damned railway track and start looking for a major road. We're bound to meet the army or at least find some ruddy transport.'

Here Voytek added his bit of wisdom: 'One snag lads, most of this shower seem to have the same idea. If there is anything going let's be there first.'

On this we all agreed. We started off with the rising sun over our shoulders across typical plain of central Poland where cultivated land from horizon to horizon is only occasionally speckled by tall silver birches and drooping willows. Above, the daily concerto of skylarks, obviously unaware of hostilities, began announcing their presence in the warming sun-rays. Although we carried hardly any luggage it soon became apparent that in the heat of the day drink will be a major problem. As we progressed through field after field I noticed that Rafal developed a limp and was beginning to suffer but he stayed quiet like the rest of us.

'What's up with your leg Raf, athlete's foot?' I inquired jokingly.

'Don't be brainless,' was the reply, 'I must have twisted this ankle jumping from the train, it's not too bad.'

We continued westwards, slowing down with every hour until by midday with no other soul in sight we dropped down exhausted and dehydrated in the shade of a lonely birch between another wheat field and acres and acres of potatoes. Something had to be said and it came from Zbych whose brain still showed some signs of activity as he began to think aloud: ' . . . if there are potatoes there must be a farm not far away . . . spuds need looking after . . . and where there is farm there is water, prawda?' We staggered to our feet. Above the shimmering heat one lonely skylark continued his song which at this time sounded more like prophecy of doom. Working our way around the never ending potato field we detected at last a sign of human presence. Across the shallow ditch my disbelieving eyes found a cheering sight of recently used cart track. Excited I turned to my lagging companions: 'Look what I found! This track must lead somewhere, let's go.' Alas, it took nearly two frustrating kilometers before we reached the dusty country road. Looking south, between some big spreading trees one could just distinguish thatched roofs of a smallholding. Dying of thirst, covered in mixture of sweat and encrusted dust we arrived at the gate of a garden separating two cottages to an eerie silence and no sign of life. Voytek opened the gate. Rusty, squeaky hinges woke up a nasty sounding dog somewhere behind the houses. Gingerly we moved forward past the hollyhocks and daisies when an old man appeared in the doorway. Bent nearly in half and heavily wrinkled he carefully examined the unexpected visitors. His croaky voice tried to overcome continuous barking in the background.

'And what are you boys doing here in these parts?' he inquired.

'Before we explain anything,' I pleaded, 'please may we have some water . . . we're completely dried up.'

'Sure, sure, the well is just around the corner.'

'But what about the dog?' asks Zbych pointing at the snarling hound.

'Oh, don't worry about him, he's tied up.'

I do not remember who got to the well first except that it was not Rafal. His right ankle was now badly swollen and his shoe must have given him hell. Nevertheless, he managed to join us in uninhibited joy of drinking and dousing ourselves with buckets of freshest cool water I have ever tasted. Our ancient host crept up towards us. He seemed to take pleasure from this sudden activity in his yard and shouted at the dog to shut up. Meanwhile two buxom middle-aged women emerged from the low doorway between two cottages, dressed in traditional peasant attire with colourful pinnies prominent, their weather-beaten faces gaping at the spectacle. They disappeared just as quickly when Zbych decided to take his trousers off. At last, having satisfied our thirst we began to explain misfortunes of the day and inquired politely if there was any food available for the starving mouths.

'We can pay you for it,' I said eagerly.

'You do no such thing, there is plenty for all of us here.' The old man seemed hurt by the offer, his faded blue eyes trying to focus in my direction. 'Guest home, God home,' he added with dignity.

An hour later, after resting our legs on most conveniently placed bales of hay by the barn door and stomachs growling with hunger, we sat at the spotless pine wood table filling our plates from a massive bowl of kasha and chomping on fresh, dark and delicious farm bread. Although I have eaten kasha in small amounts before, I have never thought it could taste so good. It is essentially a country dish, made with buckwheat, dried mushrooms and bits of various meats but once upon a time it graced, so I was told, the royal tables of Polish kings. Well, I was not impressed until now. Even so there was no chance of us having second helpings despite the persistence of two attentive dears. Full to the brim Voytek leaned towards me: 'Have you ever seen anything like it,' he asked quietly, 'these people must be from another planet.' I agreed.

Outside it was getting dark. Old Mateus, for that was his name, brought an oil lamp which must have remembered Napoleonic wars and placed it carefully in the middle of our table. He obviously noticed Rafal's bare and swollen ankle and pointed to it with his stick. 'You better get this seen to, young man, our Gabrynia is good with anything like that.' Soon enough Gabrynia arrived with metres of cheese cloth and a pot of what looked and smelled like goose grease. While the operation commenced and my reluctant brother began to relax, another unhappy tale unfolded of families parting and neglect of once proud estate which was as large and prosperous as any in the whole of Poland. The worst of it happened weeks ago when all fit men, including Squire Zamoyski, were recalled to active service and the children and most mothers were moved to Zamosc, the squire's town developement with a school and hospital. Transport became main problem in these parts after horses were commandeered by the army. 'That's easy to believe,' I said, 'since we walked all day without seeing any movement. We better save our legs and energy for tomorrow. I wonder how far it is to the main road?'

Mateus hesitated for a while weighing his words with care. 'It must be best part of five viorsts and if you turn left by the cross it goes all the way to Lvov, they say, how far I don't know.' Armed with such discouraging information I looked around and found nothing but resignation in the tired faces.

We settled for the night in the adjacent byre and slept in comfort on bed of springy, fresh smelling hay in close proximity to a cow opposite. It seemed most unfair, therefore, to be awakened at some ghastly hour to the sounds of a trumpeting cockrel and an equally noisy response from the guardian dog. Voytek already on his feet was making a clumsy attempt at milking the cow when Gabrynia arrived with half filled bucket of sour milk and a large loaf. She examined Rafal's ankle and shook her head in disapproval: 'No way can you, my son, walk on this today,' she declared. Of course, we have already expected such a verdict but no one wished to upset the sad looking patient any further and nothing was said until now. 'Well, what the hell,' said Zbych, 'we all deserve a bit of rest and there is nothing wrong with this hotel, is there lads?'

My brother was visibly relieved by this offer of comradeship and I was also grateful but the nagging thoughts of frustration and shattered plans remained. Poor Raf, I reflected, ever since early childhood, although eighteen months older, seemed to play a second fiddle to my carefree existence. Severely handicapped from the beginning when exceptionally short sighted vision in a small boy caused him to persevere with thick rimmed glasses, he also had to encounter a most miserable stroke of bad fortune at the age of ten when doctors diagnosed para-typhoid shortly after a visit to annual county fair. I still remembered how he nearly died in the arms of our mother after a serious operation on his infected chest which left him with an eight inch scar under the left shoulder blade. Recovery was slow and tedious from practically a skeleton to a slim, tall and rather studious looking teenager. Meanwhile, left to myself, I pursued everything from childish games to skiing and skating during our long, crisp and snowy winters. My reports from the junior school in

Vilno, where my father as City Commandant was stationed during those trying days, must have made pathetic reading yet no one seemed to notice. I was grateful to my brother for that. As years went by my progress of growing up concentrated mainly on the unhindered ability to participate in just about every sport available and not surprisingly Rafal had to find more intelectual pursuits such as village maidens to stay in the race. 'Chalk and cheese,' our auntie Zofja used to say, 'it's hard to believe they come from the same parents!'

Under strict orders from the two females Rafal spend the rest of our extended stay relaxing and watching us stow bales of hay into the cowshed, chop wood and fill big, rusty tank with water for the animals. Old Mateus was most grateful and I had a feeling he would not mind us staying a good deal longer.

Next morning, well fed and watered, we were saying farewells to our generous hosts whose God-fearing and sad existence was such a contrast to that of city dwellers. Rafal's foot, neatly bandaged and protected by an improvised leather sandal, seemed to perform fine at the outset but the distance of 5 viorsts described by Mateus was viewed, to say the least, with suspicion and no one was particularly cheerful. It took, in fact, three hours of steady plodding to reach a minor potholed road braced by two continuous rows of tall poplars where we sat down on the edge waiting for a minor miracle. The most nagging and depressing thoughts at this stage were about the complete lack of information in a volatile war situation with an added feeling of helplessness. Even Zbych ran out of ideas and conversation was sparse. Suddenly, a distant sound of an engine brought us all to our feet.

'Something's coming, something's coming!' rang out excited voices.

A military Fiat jeep with six occupants, unshaven and covered in dust, pulled up in response to our frantic waving.

'What the hell are you doing here,' bellowed a man next to the driver.

'We're trying to find and join any army unit,' I said.

He looked at me with pity, 'Forget it son ... it's all over. The Gerry is already this side of Vistula or didn't you know?' We shook our heads in disbelief.

'Could be only a matter of hours before they are here, our orders are to head for Chernovitze on Rumanian border,' he continued, ' . . . most of the regiment was wiped out near Czestochowa . . . you better do the same, there are few more vehicles behind us, there may be room for you lot if you want to run that is . . .' I looked at Rafal and the lads. They seemed as shocked as I was.

'Just a moment, please sir,' I noticed rank of a Captain on the dirt covered shoulder, 'could you not take at least my brother here,' I pointed to Rafal's ankle, 'he's injured his leg.'

The officer took a long look at the back of packed vehicle and relented.

'Very well, shove him inside between the seats.' This we did without a chance of saying goodbye even as the jeep accelerated down the road.

As dust settled in the distance it was time to take stock.

'It looks like a long walk,' suggested Zbych, 'unless you feel like forming a welcoming party for the bloody Germans.'

I picked up the satchel and slung it over my shoulder, 'At least we still have some food, and the Captain did say there were others behind him.'

My attempt at improving our shattered morale did not bring much cheer to Voytek as he stood up, streched himself to full size of a giant that he was, muttering nasty things about his fate and doubting parenthood of the enemy.

By early afternoon, at a steady pace, we must have covered nearly 20 kilometers, frequently looking back in vain for some friendly sign of life, but nothing came. The countryside started taking a different shape with hills appearing on the horizon and green clusters of trees replacing endless fields of golden corn. Tired, shirts saturated with sweat, we finally fell on the bed of pine needles under a large spruce by the roadside. Stripped to the waist I stretched out in the cooling shade realising for the first time how helpless one can feel. In morbid silence I watched a trail of ants labouring seemingly without any purpose up and down the tree trunk. No more talk of victory or great Allies in the West, confidence and optimism gone only one thing remained and that was will to survive. Mercifully my thoughts vanished at the long awaited sound of an engine. To everyone's surprise it did not come from behind but some distance ahead and after increasing in volume for a while it faded slowly out of hearing.

'What do you make out of that,' I asked jumping to my feet.

'Could be the Gerry,' says Voytek trying to hide behind the branches. Zbych and I were not put off, 'Don't you be stupid lad, unless we find out we won't know, will we now? Get your kit together and let's move.'

Voytek, as usual, did not contradict his mate's decisions. He lifted his enormous shoes and changed the subject. 'Look at these holes, I hope they last another day.'

'If they don't we'll have to look for two canoes,' Zbych, already on his way, shouted back.

The road was now rising, winding its way to the shallow ridge covered completely by a thick blanket of cultivated forest. This sight reduced our apprehension greatly feeling less exposed to potential enemy. Soon after reaching top of the rise and no more than few hundred meters ahead a big surprise, major road ahead! Sneaking our way through the trees we reached the crossroads and waited for something to happen. Within minutes two military trucks roared past heavily laden with gear and troops. There was no doubt about their Polish markings or uniforms. 'HURRAH! We made it at last!' I exploded waiting in vain for similar reaction from my friends.

'So what, big deal,' grunted Zbych, 'It's no use to us, is it?'

'Well, it is better than walking for days . . . and did we not set out to meet with them in the first place?' I added hastily.

'It's too bloody late for all that lad, and who is going to stop for us anyway.' We waved at another passing car without success. 'See what I mean? It's getting dark, time to look for somewhere to bed in, God knows what tomorrow might bring.'

Hurt and deflated I trailed behind my companions when Voytek, some distance ahead, showed first signs of excitement for days. 'Hey, look what I found!' He stood on the stone wall of a small bridge over a most inviting stream of gurgling water pointing at the thick undergrowth below.

'Good for you, at least we can have a bath,' laughed Zbych.

'No, no, see this turn off from the road where it disappears in the bushes?' We looked anxiously into fast fading shadows. 'I think, I could see a car there . . . I am sure I did.'

This time I was first down the lane which must have been created for the benefit of weary travellers and thirsty horses. To my astonishment Voytek was right as I nearly collided with a big black and obviously abandoned limousine no more than 20 meters from the bridge. After the initial agitation we settled down in total darkness on luxurious leather upholstery and finished the last of smoked pork and bread unable even to appreciate good fortune bestowed upon us. With no sound of movement on the road our souls quickly succumbed to bewitching silence outside and badly needed sleep ended another exhausting day.

I woke up somewhat disorientated by slamming of car's doors, excitable voices and strange knocking under the bonnet.

'I tell you there is nothing wrong with this bus, look down here, no sign of rust, engine turns over, these Packards cost a fortune.'

'Then why doesn't the ruddy thing start apart from the fact that there is no key to it.'

'Just give me half an hour and I'll find out, meanwhile shut up and keep your fingers crossed.'

As I emerged into fresh air all that could be seen of Zbych was his backside poking from underneath the bonnet. I followed Voytek who was already by the stream trying to decide whether to risk a wash or not. 'Jesus Christ, that's freezing,' he yelled withdrawing his wet hand.

'Don't be such a weakling, man. Have you seen the colour of your feet? I am sure you wouldn't like to travel looking like this in our limousine if we ever get it going again.'

My teasing hit a tender spot. 'You sound like a bloody matron, Posh Boy, try it yourself!' Cold, crystal clear water of the stream was indeed paralising first thing in the morning and I had to use all my will power not to submit as I gingerly immersed my own extremities. Watching me suffer, Voytek's cheeky smile reappeared. Inadvertently, I began to feel part of the team for the first time.

We arrived back at the car in a much better mood extolling quality of our refreshing experience suggesting to Zbych that he should do the same before we start walking again. 'Don't be bloody silly,' was the reply, 'there is nothing wrong with this engine I tell you. I could start it with this wire connection if there was only a drop of petrol in the tank.' He looked at us without a hope of an answer. 'Come on, Brains, where do we find it?' Confronted by blank faces Zbych tried his own initiative. 'Let's see what's happening on the road.'

So far, since daylight, we heard only one vehicle go past and now apart from bubbling water under the bridge and few accompanying birds there was an enchanting tranquillity all around with no sign of movement. Our mechanic outstretched his arms in desperation: 'Does anybody know there is a war going on? You two stay here and shout like hell if you see anything approaching, I am going for a dip.'

It was nearly eight o'clock before we espied the first vehicle, a single horse drawn peasant cart with four women on board. We wished them good morning and sat down on the parapet again. Zbych joined us looking more like a human being again but still ready to fight the windmills. 'Don't bother with any private cars, only lorries or army trucks are likely to carry spare fuel.'

'But we haven't seen a darn thing so far, large or small, we could be wasting our time.' My patience was now at a low ebb.

'Well, see it this way,' he continued unperturbed, 'the Captain said Gerries are already on this side of Vistula, likely it cost them a bloody nose but just you wait till they get a second wind, you won't be able to cross this road.'

Miraculously, although his assumption was later proven wrong, by mid morning traffic began to pile up. Several early arrivals roared past without paying much attention to our waving but soon things slowed down and now and again came even to a grinding halt. This opportunity was not to be missed by my companions and after few unsuccessful attempts they were engaged in frantic conversation with the uniformed driver of a requisitioned lorry who seemed quite receptive to the story related in a most appealing style by Zbych. I heard only a word or two from where I stood but I was sure doctor and orphanage were mentioned. Result: 40 litre can of petrol! I could hardly believe my eyes as Voytek arrived bearing the heavy load and equally large smile right across his cherub face.

'How did he do it? What on earth did he tell them?' I kept asking without getting any joy.

'One day we'll tell you,' they teased.

We took turns in priming the heavy engine but without enormous strength of our juvenile Hercules nothing would have induced the Packard to start. Yet, start it did after several loud bangs and a cloud of blue smoke from the rear. Happiness was complete and I thought that Zbych was a genius. He reversed the car back on the road and squeezed into two lanes of traffic like an expert. Sitting in comfort of our unexpectedly acquired limousine was such a contrast to the recent hardships that we did not notice absence of food till pangs of hunger that afternoon reminded us of other things besides pleasures of motoring. Some pleasures! Stuck between a lorry and another requisitioned bus full of soldiers we managed 50 kilometers in six hours, about half distance to Chernovice. All that way we passed only one village and a few cottages with hardly any signs of occupants. It was definitely time to eat. Between a clump of trees a small hamlet appeared ahead on our right and at the sight of chickens and geese feeding by a small pond Zbych pulled up to investigate. We managed to get a stale loaf of bread and a small piece of cheese for which I had to pay with the few remaining zlotys. While the transaction was going on, Voytek disappeared temporarily but turned up as we were ready to go and jumped on the back seat holding tightly to his bulging jacket and looking around rather suspiciously. 'Let's get the hell out of here,' he whispered and we did not ask any questions. It turned out to be a large chicken very much expired with a brocken neck which gave us sustenance for the next 24 hours after being expertly spit roasted by the roadside a few kilometers further on. Not able to operate the car's lights without the ignition key we pulled up off the road before dark with still at least twenty kilometers from the Rumanian border. Just before sunrise on 17th September Zbych managed to force his way back into a tightly packed double queue of vehicles full of unsmiling and anxiously staring faces. The impending seriousness of our situation hit us with full reality few hours later when, in sight of the border post, two Polish frontier guards, unarmed but still in uniform,waved us down begging for a lift.

'Hop in, what's happening out there?'

'Haven't you heard? Bloody Russians have crossed our border, masses of them, can't be too far now, how is that for a stab in the back!'

Mouths wide open and beginning to shake with trepidation we counted every meter to the post swearing at the slow progress. Fortunately, the Rumanian guards confronted with an impossible task of sorting out formalities in such a chaotic pile up, stood back wondering what had hit them. We crossed the frontier at 9 a.m. in company of thousands shattered and openly sobbing compatriots. Both sides of the road were braced now by two columns of foot weary civilians slogging under the weight of salvaged possessions who must have made their way towards the frontier during the past few days probably still hoping they would not have to cross it after all. Watching this byproduct of a first ever blitzkrieg was an experience more shocking by its swiftness and scale of upheaval than anyone could expect and I found it impossible to comprehend on that terrible day. Our Packard was filled now to capacity with a few more bodies and their belongings whose emotional gratitude visibly embarassed Zbych, doubtless for the first time ever. Sitting next to him I also found it difficult to conceal my feelings, especially not being used to crying since the age of six.

'Easy, Sonny Boy, think how lucky you are,' he said slowly through the corner of his mouth, 'what do you think would happen to a son of a Colonel if the bastard Bolshevicks got hold of him . . . 10 years in Siberia minimum, I reckon.'

That sobering thought soon brought me back to reality. At the same time somebody outside shouted through the open window: 'They've just closed the border!' I looked at my watch. It was now exactly one hour since we crossed the Chernovitze check point.

CHAPTER 2

From Exile To Exile

Our massive convoy continued through the Moldavian valley on a road winding along banks of river Siret until early afternoon when things were reduced to a crawl again. On reaching the first crossroads we found Rumanian soldiers directing traffic and discovered that someone at last knew where we were likely to finish. Using German as the only common language, I was told that we were to follow all civilian vehicles already assembled ahead of us to a camp 20 kilometers away and that we must part with our two uniformed guards. Eventually our much reduced convoy was on the way once more, this time up a narrow track climbing steeply into the forests of Carpathian mountains with breath taking views on both sides. To our surprise and great relief the camp turned out to be more of a holiday resort on the slopes of a picturesque dale with prefabricated chalets clustering beneath giant beeches. The place was called Calimanesti and in the centre of it a large corrugated shed advertised food and drink. Needless to say my two charlatans decided that this was the paradise they were waiting for and within minutes not only found an empty part of a chalet with camping beds provided, but also persuaded three of our ever grateful passengers to part with some foreign currency which, in view of my bankruptcy, they thought essential.

A few days went by during which all the remaining Rumanian holiday makers departed, pressurised by overcrowding, noise and also probably by the queues outside the only latrine, which even on our arrival one could recognise by its powerful smell from behind the vertical hessian drapery. The weather remained fine although

17

slightly cooler at this height which suited me fine on the long hikes and wild mushroom searches, the aroma of which when cooked was equalled only by their exquisite taste. I simply could not believe that the upheaval I had lived through only days before could finish in such idyllic and peaceful surroundings. 'If this is war let me have more of it,' Voytek kept repeating. Yet, reality was much more different back home. Greedy invaders had split Poland in two, obviously by prior agreement between Hitler and Stalin. A non-aggression pact now acquired new and sinister meaning. Warsaw's heroic defenders fired their last bullets and finally on 29th September German storm troopers marched into the centre of a ruined city.

We were heading now for the arrival of autumn heralded by gradual change in nature, and here in the Rumanian forest, by the spectacular transformation of colours around us. Mountain slopes began to display large areas of gold and bright orange where magnificent beeches contrasted with the dark green of equally tall pines and invited any onlooker to get nearer. My pent up worry, particularly about my mother left behind caring for her disabled father, my total frustration and helplessness, took me daily on long treks into the unspoiled wilderness of Carpathians where the surroundings suitably matched my loneliness. Luckily, one afternoon, a completely unexpected occurrence far more therapeutic than my physical labours send me tumbling into a new and fascinating world.

It was while returning from another day of exploration that I met Irka. Startled at first by presence of another human being in the narrow gorge which I considered practically my own property, I stood rooted to the spot after the vision of a beautiful girl slid down from a craggy rock almost into my arms and jumped back even quicker, clearly shocked by the experience. We stared at each other for a while in silence then uttered a few apologies which were evidently not needed except for the realisation that we used the same language. I was too mesmerised by her loveliness to start any conversation and felt an idiot. Seeing my embarrassment she smiled and spoke first. 'Are you from the camp?' Her voice sounded like music. I nodded my head.

'When did you arrive?'

'Two weeks ago.'

'Are you with your family?'

'No. Are you?'

She introduced herself. 'My name is Irka, I came here with my mother after we managed to escape from Lvov before the Russians came,' she smiled again while I continued staring at her parted lips.

'Is there something wrong with me?' she asked looking down shyly.

'Oh no, of course not,' I hurried to reassure her, 'I am Jacek, I came from Warsaw.' Losing some of my bashfulness I suggested we should start for home before sunset. She seemed quite relaxed now and chattered all the way back to the camp relating her dull existence here, without friends and not even a book to read.

'That's why I came so far today hoping to find some hazel nuts. I saw people bring them from this direction but as you can see I found nothing. But I am glad I came,' she concluded giving me a quick glance from her large and lovely eyes.

I was over the moon and mustered some bravery.

'Would you like to join me tomorrow, I am pretty certain there are birches a little further on.'

'Yes, that would be nice . . . but I have to ask mum first, she does worry a lot when I go out. She doesn't seem to realise that I am nearly seventeen and can look after myself.'

We stopped outside an ivy covered bungalow and she pointed at the door. 'This is where we stay with three other unaccompanied women refugees,' she paused for a moment, 'but I will do my best for tomorrow. What time do you normally set off?'

'Whenever it suits you, say 8 o'clock, here?'

My heart was afloat and I felt like jumping over every fence on the way back to our hut. Voytek and Zbych watched me with great suspicion that evening and it was not very long before the penny dropped. My happy glowing face, disregard of their company and sudden loss of appetite must have been a give away.

'Just look at him, I bet he's found a popsy. Is she nice?'

As I blushed the teasing continued. 'You lucky bastard, it's not easy to find a bit of crumpet in this Transylvanian wilderness unless she's Dracula's daughter!'

They both burst out laughing but I was too blissful to be annoyed. Anyway, my thoughts seemed incapable of changing direction as I laid on my bunk struck by the very first experience of love sickness. It was probably more serious because of our family's inability to produce daughters, that is, ever since granddad Blocki married a Hungarian beauty and engineered five sons, who in turn increased population of males in southern Poland on a grand scale. Such a state of affairs continued for over sixty years and when I arrived on the scene my knowledge of the opposite sex was restricted to my mother Wanda and her sister Zofia. The latter being childless took upon herself to spoil me wickedly which I enjoyed on the quiet but pretended otherwise. Even at school all my tutors turned out to be males and the classroom full of masochistic sport-mad boys left me only with love affairs of book heroines such as portrayed by Prus or those in an uncensored version of Emil Zola which was smuggled into the classroom during my last term. If anything up to now, I found women frightening. No wonder my delightful experience that day in Calimanesti left me sleepless, floating as if through heavenly clouds.

Early next morning I sneaked outside without breakfast and waited at our rendezvous for only few minutes before Irka arrived. We were both half an hour early and it should have been apparent that such keenness was not prompted by hazel nuts.

However, this kind of reasoning never occurred to us as we departed hand in hand. A few hesitant words later and out of sight of the village she suddenly stopped, turned towards me, her open arms reaching for my face and kissed me. It was the longest two seconds I have experienced in the whole of my seventeen years. My lips seemed in contact with magnetic silk. Before I could regain any semblance of earthly presence she stepped back hiding her face behind golden brown tresses and whispered coyly, 'I wanted to do this since yesterday . . . I thought you would be my boy friend for always . . .'

Now I knew I was in heaven.

For the following two weeks Irka spent much time in my arms while we chose to forget the world and its troubles, discovering first love, touching, caressing and whispering sweet nothings. Yet, all that time the troubles around us were mounting. The sudden arrival of a Polish official from the Bucharest Embassy finally acted on all of us like a cold shower.

The Rumanian government, threatened and pressurised by the Germans, had abandoned their softly-softly policy towards Poles. This meant that all males of arm bearing age had to be removed within days to internment camps to prevent the steady drift of escaped soldiery westwards, aided and abetted by the remains of Polish consular staff in Bucharest. We should expect therefore to say good-bye to our freedom as soon as our hosts found sufficient transport. 'Bloody charming!' growled Zbych supported by the gathered throng of worried faces. 'And where are they going to take us from here?' The surrounded diplomat shrugged his shoulders but promised to help anyone who could make Bucharest under his own steam.

During the next two days anxiety reigned throughout the camp. As for myself my whole world turned topsy-turvy; on one side dreading any thought of departure from the enchanted fairyland of Irka's company and on the other unable to resist the compelling urge to carry out my patriotic duty. In a nutshell, to join our Forces in France. Zbych and Voytek, crafty as they were, could not find an immediate solution to our predicament either, since all our vehicles including the Packard were removed by soldiers soon after we arrived in Calimanesti and no one fancied foot slogging across Rumanian mountains. On the third morning, as predicted, a motley crowd of soldiers arrived in a lorry followed by two ancient buses. Unarmed, except for an officer and his crony bearing four chevrons on each sleeve, they appeared more like refugees than we did. I wondered if they would consider me too young for military service but anything in trousers seemed to satisfy their mission. Irka clung to me till the last minute while we exchanged promises of eternal love no matter how long it took to fulfil our dreams. Little did we know then how unpredictable our future was in the forthcoming turmoil of the world war and even less the realisation that this also applied to a vast number of humanity.

The old bus rattled noisily in a convoy of four vehicles along the potholes of Transylvanian roads for the rest of that day. I sat by a dirty, cracked window hardly able to notice the most intriguing landscape, so often copied in the Hollywood horror films. Inside me, a feeling of emptiness and resignation left my mind stunned, incapable of sharing thoughts or conversation. My Warsaw friends however kept their eyes and ears wide open and even managed to engage four sleepy guards in a conversation using arms, fingers and feet as well as few words of unknown origin, occasionally to the amusement of otherwise poker faced passengers. Late in the afternoon we entered the streets of a sizable town. Our bus rattled past a market place surrounded by rows of tiny shops which displayed on the outside everything from pots and pans to clothing. 'I could do business here,' said Zbych, 'I wonder how far we have to go yet.' It so happened he did not have to wait long. It was only two kilometers further on when our convoy staggered to a halt facing large iron gates of a compound surrounded by barbed-wire fence. Once inside we were firmly but politely introduced to a long wooden hut and rows of double bunks filled with straw. Sanitation was again beyond any civilised description and the whole camp oozed uniformly with the combined aroma of the ablutions and the adjacent cookhouse. As we settled for the night I could not contain myself any longer.

'We have to get out of here fast,' I whispered to Voytek in the next bunk.

'Did you hear that,' he turned to Zbych below him, 'I think our lad is waking up at last.'

'It's about ruddy time. We'll make a recce tomorrow, sleep well.' During the next 24 hours we discovered the following:

a) Our internment camp was called Targoviste after the market town we had seen earlier.

b) The only guards, who were changed every four hours throughout the day and night, consisted of two soldiers. They usually leant on the gates and showed complete lack of enthusiasm for their jobs.

c) Apart from a vehicle compound full of the Polish military transport, which was confined for the duration, most of the fencing was in need of repair. In places loose wire left gaps big enough for a giant to get through.

By a coincidence and to my great relief I found out also from some other inmates that my brother Rafal had made it across the border and had been seen in another camp near Brasov well to the north of us.

After hours of discussing several clandestine plans my two pals decided on the third evening to venture out and see if anything was on offer on the other side of the fence. I waited till the middle of the night in a state of nervous tension expecting nothing but trouble, tossing and turning in my bunk, when out of the shadows unmistakable figure of Voytek appeared followed closely by Zbych. Both seemed in a good mood and, from their whispered experiences outside, I gathered that whatever plan they had it had been created by optimistic minds.

Two weeks went by. It was middle of November now and first rains came and went, bringing cold winds from the mountains adding to the general misery of the camp's inhabitants. Some of the earlier arrivals managed to disappear in mysterious circumstances while others were brought in from all over Rumania. The local authorities either lost count or did not care. Shocking tales of cruelty and barbaric treatment of Poles by occupying Soviet forces came with the refugees, none worse than one related by a 16 year old boy who arrived with his arms in plaster after jumping from a Siberian bound train full of slave labour. These victims of Stalin's ruthlessness had been sentenced by 'People's' courts, established within days of the Russian occupation throughout the country. The young man had been accused of being a policeman's son, which he did not deny, and without any further ado was sentenced to 5 years of hard labour by a middle aged female prosecutor who sat between two uniformed officers. In the absence of any defence one of the older accused present started to plead on behalf of the boy.

'How can you call it justice, please, have a heart, he's only a lad . . .'

Visibly, this naive interruption created a most unwelcome challenge to the woman's authority for she jumped to her feet and started shouting across the court towards the offender.

'And who do you think you are, you son of a prostitute, we have seven million do-gooders like you under lock and key!' She raised herself above the desk and lifted her skirt chest high, 'Take a good look,' her voice throbbing with fury, 'you're not going to see it for ten years, you Polish bastard! Take him away!'

On the other side of the Vistula Hitler's S.S. thugs were executing dissidents and preparing ghettos for the Polish Jews. Naturally, such events registered deeply in my wounded soul. Although unnoticed at first, the transformation from a young idealist to an angry and hardened individual was already taking place. Privation coupled with the miserable conditions which I found myself in did not help my intellect either. I learned a variety of swear words which I had never heard before, and mastered an art of breaking wind in public to the amusement of recipients. In the meantime Zbych and Voytek, having made three more illegal excursions into town, were ready to implement their plan of escape and I was more than ready to join them.

Our attention focused on the adjacent car park. From one of the Targoviste traders, a wily Jew who could speak Russian and a little Polish, the boys discovered that while petrol was ridiculously cheap in Rumania, such things as pneumatic tyres were a price of gold. 'If you could get me a set from one of your jeeps I may help you to buy your way out of this hole,' he suggested. All we needed, according to Zbych, was a wire cutter, a monkey-wrench and a dark night. The first two were supplied without payment by Voytek after another visit to the market. The same night when all seemed quiet we sneaked into the farthest corner from our gate guardians, where I watched, with a good deal of admiration, the art of breaking and entering with hardly a squeak to be heard. After half an hour of keeping a look out a faint whisper behind the barbed wire sounded almost too loud. 'Here, come through and give us a hand.'

We lifted each corner of the Fiat in turn while all four wheels were taken off and quietly deposited in thick bushes on the outside of the vehicle compound. Back in our bunks we congratulated ourselves on a job well done leaving the disposal of hidden booty till next evening. What we underestimated, however, was the weight of each wheel. Because we had no means of separating tyres from the rims, each had to be carried complete over rough fields and the whole operation took two nights. However, as we laid exhausted early on the third day, it was very satisfying to know that under the straw rested a veritable loot of lira, the local currency one counted in thousands, as well as a timetable of buses to Bucharest. There was no time to waste now and as darkness fell we collected our shabby belongings and hit the Targoviste trail for the last time.

It is almost impossible to describe our elation after the half empty bus we boarded set off along the bumpy road. Fortunately, our appearance, apart from the happy faces, seemed to match that of other passengers and no one paid much attention to another untidy lot of peasants. The journey took two hours and I gathered that by the time we arrived in the middle of Bucharest, well before midnight, our bus had struggled for only 30 to 40 kilometers. Bright lights, the sight of pavements, pedestrians and busy street traffic has not been experienced since Warsaw and we stood wide-eyed for quite some time before Zbych, as usual, brought us back to reality.

'I'll be damned, never expected such living in this arse hole of a country, look at all the taxies flying by.'

'So what,' I chipped in, 'have we got enough money to eat, never mind the taxies?'

'We'll soon find out,' said he hailing one to a stop. 'How much to hotel . . . er, pension?'

Confronted by a blank face, Zbych took out a wad of banknotes and waved it in front of the driver's face. While his eyes lit up at the sight of money his mouth did not make any sense to us. I tried some simple German. 'Wieviel nach eine kleine Pension?'

'Ah, Ich ferstehe, ein hundert bitte.' This sorted out, we discovered to our amazement that with thousands of lira in our pockets we could afford a decent style of life for a while. Our small hotel provided a badly needed shower, bed, sheets and flush toilet on each of its three floors. Seeing what seemed like luxury after our ordeal we certainly did not mind paying for two nights in advance. The weedy looking landlord pocketed the money and introduced us to his grossly over-weight wife. She found it too much of an effort to lift her wobbly frame out of a well worn settee but assured us that her culinary skills were the best in Bucharest. Next morning we found her breakfast pretty ordinary but no one dared to complain. Number one priority now was to acquire some warm clothing for all the remains of our summer attire were in shreds and Voytek's shoes had gaps like crocodile's jaws. In fact, it took us hours to find a pair for his enormous feet but in the end Zbych and I were rewarded with a beaming smile. Next on the list had to be a visit to our Embassy. Another taxi was hailed. We arrived in a quiet residential street facing a less impressive building than the name outside it would suggest. Between neglected flower beds, a footpath covered by fallen autumn leaves led to wooden double doors badly in need of re-painting. Even before crossing the threshold I had an insecure feeling that the occupiers were not preparing for an indefinite stay. Inside we joined a queue of at least 20 men waiting to enter one of the rooms at the end of a lengthy corridor. After an hour two fellows walked out of the office followed by an official who announced that no more business would be carried out until next morning. Nothing complimentary was said between us on the way back but we did learn from other sufferers that in due time they do issue temporary passports and even tickets to foreign destinations. Left with nothing to do for the rest of that day I spent the evening in my room under a cloud of depressing thoughts, unable to erase memories of Irka, my family or my disintegrated country.

It was still dark when, confronted by a good deal of abuse, I tried to get my companions out of bed. 'Right,' I said, 'stay here if you want to but unless you get your lousy bodies outside in five minutes you can stay here for ever!' Eventually, I had to wait half an hour but it worked. Clever as they were in some respects the thought of dealing with an interview had them both obviously worried.

In the same corridor we found ourselves this time in front of the queue but still had to wait mid-morning before the officials arrived. My reluctant heroes pushed me in through an opened door wondering no doubt what shock treatment was in store inside. The two gentlemen supported by a typist must have done this chore a hundred times before and after writing down my name, they did not waste much time on small talk.

'Where were you born?'

'Rzeszow.'

'How old are you?'

'Eighteen this month.'

'Any means of identification?'

I pulled out my school identity card, 'This is the only thing I have.' Both men studied the card and my photo and whispered to each other before one spoke in a much more relaxed manner.

'So you want to join the army?'

'Yes, sir.'

'You are rather young, still, by the time you arrive in France they will be ready for you. We shall prepare your passport and travel documents. Bring your photographs today and be ready to move next week. Anywhere to stay?'

'Yes, thank you, I share a room with two friends. They are waiting outside.'

He opened the desk drawer, counted carefully some paper money and handed the notes to me. 'Here, this should tie you over for a few days and remember, not a word to any one about this, certainly not in public. German spies are crawling all over this city.'

On the way out I turned around, happiness written all over my face, thanking them both loudly. Maybe I should have paid more attention then to a sombre 'Don't mention it' from behind the desk, but I did not.

In the corridor I met the all-inquiring eyes and ears. 'Piece of cake,' I announced proudly but Zbych and Voytek were not impressed. I left them by the dreaded door to seek a photographer and returned before lunch with horrible, faint images of myself in quadruplicate. I found my pals sitting outside by a dried up well in the Embassy's garden with faces as long as could be and not showing any enthusiasm at my arrival. 'What's wrong lads?' I inquired and received couple of groans in reply. After some coaxing it became clear that their passage through the bureaucratic network was as rough as they expected. The fact that they had no means of identification, no permanent address in Poland and could hardly sign their names must have had something to do with this and I immediately offered to vouch for their origin and even integrity.

'Never mind that,' said Zbych sadly, 'they tried to tell us it was too late to check our credentials, whatever that means, for the next shipment so we have to wait. I think they want better quality gun fodder. Is this why you're going next week, you toffee nosed son of a bitch?'

There was no answer to that but before I could open my mouth he got up and grabbed me with both arms. 'Don't take it to heart, Jacek,

I didn't mean it . . . you're not one of them,' he added.

A few days went by and after I collected the documents we celebrated my departure. This left me ill with my first ever hangover after drinking some stuff called raki. It smelled like a sewer and tasted like turpentine and even next afternoon on the platform of Bucharest railway station, I still felt extremely fragile. There were no tears as I entered the Constanza bound train but Voytek did wipe his nose discretely at least twice.

'See you in France.'

'Take care Jacek,' was the last thing I heard as the train set off

It was just as well that I did not know then that I would never see either of my two guardians again. Unable to find a seat by the window I left my small suitcase to guard an empty space in the compartment and moved down the corridor for a glimpse of the Rumanian countryside. Watching the contrasting marshy plains after spectacular views of Transylvania I waited impatiently for my first view of the fabulous Danube which ends its laborious journey through the heart of Europe here. Alas, like most mighty rivers on the last lap to the sea, the Danube spills and divides into several lesser waterways, small lakes and flooded lowlands making my efforts at recognition quite futile. I pondered about ancient Romans selecting this mosquito and malaria infested country as their penal colony and was glad after two hours to sit down again and listen to the lulling clank of wheel on rail.

It was nearly dark when, surrounded by rows of petroleum tanks and huge harbour cranes, the train slowly screeched to a halt in Constanza's dockland station. There was no doubt what the main exports of this country consisted of and why the Germans kept such an interest in it. What was surprising, however, was an immediate introduction to another world called The East. Although still part of Europe, the influence of a life style from the surrounding shores of the Black Sea was unmistakable. As the carriage doors were flung open I was roughly ejected into teeming multilingual crowd on the platform which resembled a busy market place rather than a railway station. Manhandled and elbowed on the way out, I struggled past shouting porters fighting for trade, turban bearing Turks and other dark skinned types who preferred to carry their worldly possessions on their heads, while a variety of salesmen advertising everything from jewellery to money changing added to the chaos. Outside the station instant catering was on offer, mixing aromas of meats on charcoal stoves with the pungent smell of crude oil. I followed less colourful and speechless Europeans, with only few bundles or small suitcases to their name, who made slow and uncertain progress towards the quay.

Amongst them I sensed a similarity of origin and behaviour and, despite the conspicuous lack of any conversation, I rightly concluded that these fellows had received the same briefing as myself in the Polish embassy in Bucharest. We passed a number of moored ships, some seemingly held together by rust, before joining a long queue ouside a sentry box at the gates of high wired compound. It turned out to be the passport and ticket control. To my amazement there was not a Rumanian in sight and both inspectors, although in civilian clothes, spoke Polish in the military style of a Sergeant Major. In the background, just visible in fast fading daylight, was the outline of the biggest ship I have seen so far and I hoped like the rest of us that this was our transport. Once through the gates, more orders: 'Hurry, hurry you lot, you're the last bunch for this trip. We're ready to go!'

I do not think I had ever run faster in my life. I reached the narrow boarding gantry lit up now by the liner's deck lights, panting and impatient. I felt a new chapter in my life was about to begin. Pent up excitement shared by all of us finally exploded as the big ship cast off her last mooring warp and slowly edged away into the dark waters ahead. From the reception lounge, laughter and loud voices, expressing hope and happiness after days of uncertainty, drown the throbbing of the engines. I certainly did not care which cabin, berth or deck chair I was allocated and spend hours on deck that night watching mainland lights fade away in the distance and also those of passing ships which periodically appeared and dipped over the horizon. Before midnight, however, December weather began to live up to its reputation and a penetrating cold drizzle driven by an ever strengthening wind send me down below.

The same miserable wintry atmospheric conditions persisted all next day during our passage through the Bosphorus Straits, Sea of Marmara and most of Aegean Sea. Despite my proximity to this ancient and fascinating world I could hardly identify a landmark through the sea spray and low hanging clouds. In the meantime, due to the green monster of the seas, the ship's dining room remained nearly half empty. To my satisfaction I found myself one of the few who had not suffered a loss of appetite and I was even able to kill the time down below playing cards, while sympathising with the sea sick majority. Our destination was a well kept secret, creating inevitable rumours and speculation and there was no shortage of conversations on the subject. Personally, having witnessed the departure of some 500 regular soldiers and young men like myself on board just one of the ships from Constanza, I was most impressed with the scale of such clandestine operations and never really discovered who was behind them. Whoever organised, coordinated and, no doubt, bribed one or two governments to enable such a mass escape of Polish Army and Air Force personnel from the supposedly neutral countries like Rumania or Hungary should have been at least mentioned in dispatches. Especially as this was done under watchful, unfriendly and intimidating German eyes. In the company of my fellow compatriots on board, most of whom had already confronted the first blitzkrieg, I was proud that despite our defeat, the single minded common purpose of restoring free Poland was never in doubt. 'All we need now is new and better gear,' growled one prophetic, battle scarred, yet still in his twenties, veteran, 'and we'll show them!'

I thought of the two Polish regiments of horse cavalry, wiped out by the German tanks on the first day of the onslaught and could not agree more.

The second morning at sea was full of surprises. First of all we were greeted by a magnificent Mediterranean sunrise, vivid blue water and flotillas of dolphins. I felt I was in a circus and the misty distant land on our port side did not attract much attention at first. Someone close to me finally broke the spell: 'Hell fellows, we're heading East!' All faces suddenly turned towards him in disbelief as he pointed to the sun. True enough it hung just off and above the bows where most of the action had fascinated such landlubbers as myself. The land on our port side had to be Turkey and no one dared to guess where we were likely to end up. Late in the afternoon the mystery was solved with an announcement that the ship would dock in Beirut in two hours and everyone must be ready for disembarkation.

The sight of a large tricolour flying over an impressive modern harbour terminal was very reassuring as we boarded a fleet of buses waiting there. Everything was unmistakably French, from signposts, to the language of inhabitants of this western orientated city. Alas, like many other disappointments to follow, we were driven straight through for miles into the surrounding hills where a large tented camp awaited our arrival. There was not much to see in the fading daylight as we were issued with two blankets each and guided four to a tent. At first things did not look too bad as no one expected luxury and through my scouting experience as a boy I tended to ignore discomfort in the excitement of an adventure. But this was winter and at 4000 feet or more above sea level, even in Lebanon, the temperature drops frequently below freezing. My three companions, all regular soldiers and much older than myself, sorted out their camping beds and without much ado retired fully dressed for the night. Trying hard to look as casual and efficient, I followed their example although not quite as speedily. I found sleep at a premium amidst the rasping sounds of snoring which emanated from under the blankets even before I managed to take my shoes off. At 3 o'clock, after tossing and turning for hours, I realised that I was beginning to freeze and had to get up to restore my fast fading blood circulation. Outside, many voices, the stamping of feet and rubbing of hands made me realise that I was not the only sufferer. I wrapped both blankets around me and moved a few paces up and down between the beds.

'What the hell is going on? God, isn't it freezing.' The groan came from under the blanket next to me.

'Nothing is going on,' I said through my chattering teeth, 'but if you don't get up soon you'll be an ice block.'

There was a lot of swearing after that as all of my tent mates struggled to their feet groping in the dark for their blankets with shivering hands.

'To the devil with this bloody Mediterranean resort, we'll have to do something about this,' cried one.

'Lets go outside and see what the others are doing,' said another.

'They are probably shaking like us,' I suggested, 'not much can be done before daylight. Let's get our beds together, maybe we can survive close to each other sharing all the blankets.'

This we did and by morning we found ourselves still alive but angry, waiting for those responsible for our treatment. The water tap on the bowser between our tents was still frozen when two field kitchens arrived, apparently from the French army camp a few kilometers away. Long queues of disgruntled and hungry customers were created and I witnessed first breakdown of discipline in otherwise loyal troops. Not that hot black coffee, a bar of even darker chocolate and a small loaf of bread per head were unwelcome. There was a far more understandable reason for the bitching. With no officer or senior NCO in sight it became clear to the troops that they had been abandoned by their leaders.

'I bet the buggers are still asleep in those luxury hotels we saw on our way here yesterday, wait till they get here.'

'We've seen them before, haven't we? Bloody leaders from the back!'

This kind of barrack room criticism was, to say the least, disturbing to a son of an officer brought up to respect and obey his seniors and I remember walking away to contemplate the vagaries of human behaviour.

As the sun rose above the tall pines between rows and rows of camouflaged tents warmth returned to Lebanese mountains and it brought with it a more relaxed atmosphere throughout the camp. Far to the west one could just see an outline of the coast and the light blue watery horizon of the Mediterranean. Once again there was hope and a hint of optimism. After all, I had to return to keep all the promises made with such enthusiasm in front of family, pals and, most vividly, to my first love in Rumania.

Such thoughts as I entertained that morning were swiftly interrupted by the arrival of two lorries and the subsequent excitement of inmates who were awaiting impatiently for news, good or bad. As they disembarked, one Polish uniformed officer and several equally smart NCOs were immediately surrounded and followed to a large open square between the tents. Silenced eventually by a word of command we learned that this temporary camp would be our home for only three more days when a French troopship was due to arrive in Beirut. The massive cheer which greeted this statement must have been heard for miles. The next two days were completely preoccupied with the administrative business of registration, identification and documentation in the hastily arranged open air offices. Extra blankets and more nourishing food seemed to resolve any remaining rumblings and no one talked anymore about luxury hotels. I had learned my first lesson in aspects of leadership and morale.

Two days later, on 22nd December, we were told our troopship docked in Beirut and embarkation will start almost immediately. To my horror I was told at lunch time that my name was not on the list of departing soldiery. 'Don't worry son,' said the Duty Sergeant at the loading point, 'you'll be going on the next ship. They can only take so many on this run, you know, and in any case you're not the only one staying behind.'

I must admit that at this stage I did not give a damn about the others and felt abandoned once again. When the last coach rolled out down towards Beirut I returned to the empty tent and rested my deflated body, not caring what mental torture fate may produce next. Imagination began to play a few tricks. After all, Christmas is just around the corner and I can see Mamusia by the kitchen table kneading masses of dough, getting it ready for the large iron cooker in our flat in Warsaw. The mouth watering smell of sweet pastries already baking is almost unbearable but nothing will be touched until that greatest Polish religious celebration of Christmas Day. I see myself sneaking off towards the Vistula embankment, skates hanging around my neck, hoping to meet some pals on the specially watered paths that weave through acres and acres of frozen parkland. And then I fall asleep . . .

I woke up early next morning to the sound of rain splattering on canvas above me. It was soon followed by flashes of lightning, earth shaking explosions of thunder and howling gusts of wind which made my tent seem ready for take off without any further warning. I shot out of bed and miraculously found my shoes floating out of the tent. Within seconds torrential rain and sleet had flooded our campside, which was completely unprepared for such weather. The storm, however, passed over as quickly as it arrived and one hour later I was able to wander outside to observe the aftermath. Blissfully, nature's spectacular intervention made my preoccupation with personal feelings less than significant. Detailed as part of a working party, I spent the rest of that day with the remnants of camp's inmates recovering the torn out tents and digging drain trenches around those still lived in. I worked with a group of young men who like myself had nothing to do with the regular army and had been left behind as low priority individuals. Fate would have it that one of them played subsequently a major part in planning my future life. His name was Jurek. Tall with blond wavy hair and cheeky blue eyes he was nearly two years older than myself His sense of humour and a 'couldn't-care-less' attitude was badly needed after months of disappointments.

Jurek and his two pals did not wait long to invite themselves into my tent, their own having been literally blown away during the night. After supper we sorted out all our bedding, borrowing dry blankets from now abandoned tents nearby and sat down with a sigh of relief.

'How and when did you get here,' I asked.

'Do you know anything about railways?' Jurek got up to adjust the light on the hanging paraffin lantern.

'Yes, quite a bit.'

'Well, whatever you know it's peanuts to what we've been through, right lads?' As two companions nodded their heads Jurek continued, 'Apart from the comforts of a lorry from Radom to Budapest we did 1000 kilometers in cattle trucks and coal wagons from Hungary to Saloniki in three weeks. That's what you call 4th class travel. After that we took to shipping like you did, right? We have been here two weeks for our sins and now we are still waiting,' he took a deep breath, 'probably till New Year.'

'Why, do you know something about next movement,' I asked hopefully.

'You don't expect the bloody Army to tell you anything, do you, but I did overhear them chatting before they left. It appears this troopship does regular runs between here and Marseilles.'

I soon discovered the reason for such low opinion of the khaki uniforms when the origin of my companions was revealed during that evening. Last August all three of them had attended a selection board at the aircrew training centre in Deblin after passing out from their respective colleges. Jurek and Vitold were accepted by the Polish Air Force for training as pilots while Bolek, who failed on medical grounds but still chose to be near aeroplanes, volunteered for the technical branch. During the two weeks in Deblin they were treated to a couple of flights each and their enthusiasm about this and aviation in general oozed out from every sentence.

'My dear chap, you don't want to live in the past. Slogging in the trenches is as obsolete as bows and arrows! There is only one thing that can drag you out of this antiquated world and that is flying.'

I listened with eyes wide open and, impressed by such new and exciting views, I immediately wanted to find out more and more about the concept of flying.

'How does one go about joining your mob?' I inquired impatiently after more than an hour of chatter with my head in the clouds. 'Bear in mind I am not eighteen until tomorrow.'

'Don't worry about small things,' says Jurek with a grin, 'just stick with us and we will show you when time comes. By the way, what's this about your birthday tomorrow you saintly creature, it is Christmas Eve , isn't it?'

'Well, I can't help it,' I retorted trying not to make too much fuss about my age or even younger looks after many recent sarcastic remarks from my older companions.

'Anyway what difference does it make what day it is in this desert.'

Next morning we joined the breakfast queue as ordered but the boys spent more time than usual talking to the French cooks after I had wandered back to our tent. After lunch, Surprise! Vitold enters with a bulging blanket slung across his back. Out of it come two bottles of red wine, fresh rolls and a handsome chunk of gruyere cheese. Luxury indeed! As wine is poured out into tin mugs Jurek utters a few words of congratulations and the company breaks out with the traditional Polish song which wishes recipients a hundred years of life on earth. My embarrassment is complete as I sip my share of vin ordinaire hiding the mouth twisting sourness of drink fit only for the lowest ranks. The birthday party ends at sunset with chummy embraces and promises of never ending friendships but not before alcohol claims another virgin victim and I spend half an hour retching among the pines.

Christmas went by almost unnoticed and so did the New Year of 1940. After that things began to move a little. A photographer arrived and we were issued with military identity cards. We were also paid 24 francs which was two weeks back pay for Chasseur Deuxieme Classe as described in those documents. It enabled the four of us to visit the lavish city of Beirut where the cheapest cup of coffee in the Arab quarter cost 10 francs. We settled for some dates and oranges, both rather rare and expensive back in Poland. Jurek, who was desperate for a toothbrush, had to borrow two francs to pay for it and we all arrived back penniless. Despite our primitive existence we managed to develop a kind of companionship with schoolroom wit and a sense of belonging and I remember dreading the thought of ever parting from my new found friends. When, eventually, we boarded a French troopship bound for Marseilles, still together and happy once again, the hardships of Lebanon faded from our minds.

CHAPTER 3

Friends In Need

Early in the morning on 10th January we espied through low hanging mist the promised land of France. Our big ship ploughed her way slowly in still waters between weaving fishermen, their colourful craft making for the open sea, and some larger vessels at anchor before reaching Marseilles's even busier harbour. Docking seemed to take hours but no one complained while watching the manoeuvring of tugs, which I found a fascinating new experience. Once through immigration we were pointed in the direction of coaches and lorries just visible at the end of several massive storage sheds along the quay. Without any sign of welcoming or guidance the four of us clambered on board the first coach which on its windscreen advertised in large letters: POLONAISE CAMP MILITAIRE . Like the rest of occupants we beamed with excitement and chatted loudly in the atmosphere of anticipation. This turned into a good deal of humorous comment when the French drivers turned up. Our assembled convoy set off through the narrow, winding streets scattering other traffic as well as pedestrians who showed remarkable respect for the blasting horns and jumped out of the way without signs of surprise or anger. As soon as we started labourious progress uphill to the top of plateau surrounding Marseilles's coastline, our convoy was split by ever increasing number of other vehicles which also seemed to demand instant priority. Watching the speed of cars and lorries whistling past in the opposite direction I was glad that we were not travelling downhill and said so. 'Oh, don't be such a chicken,' chipped in Jurek, 'at least it would be more exciting.' I did not reply feeling somewhat inadequate in company of such placid daredevils, an attribute, which I wrongly thought then, was necessary to become a pilot. It took only few weeks in the company of youths whose enthusiasm for anything connected with aviation bordered on fanaticism to indoctrinate me in their way of thinking and act in similar way, although not always with great success.

Our high spirits of that day, due to the ignorance of realities about to confront us, would be more than needed later, in fact, as soon as we entered the portals of camp Septfont in the province of Tarn et Garonne. Behind the pretty name hid a morbid history and whoever decided to convert it into a military accommodation either had not seen it or was scraping the barrel. This was a relic of the Spanish civil war which was second to none in its barbarity. For two long years Hitler and Stalin exercised warfare at the expense of the Spanish people until General Franco assisted by the Germans crushed the Communist inspired forces. Remnants of the defeated army fled across the Pyrenees into France where they were smartly interned in such camps as Septfont while the rest of civilised world preferred to do nothing. Conditions within our camp must have been appalling. Wooden barrack in which myself and my friends were accommodated were used as a sick bay with a red cross sign still visible outside. The few blood stains which Vitold found on bunks next to his, were left probably by some poor wounded souls. Two long tables between rows of bare wooden bunks were covered with carved out Spanish names and, significantly, that of a hammer and sickle in the middle of each. There was no signs of either water taps or wash basins in the immediate vicinity but behind another barrack an overgrown path led to rectangular deep hole in the ground with heavy plank across it. This, I discovered to my horror, represented a communal toilet facility! Next to it was a primitive tin trough used for washing and laundering and the whole area stunk to high heaven. We bedded down for the night without any food after filling our mattresses with straw. Apparently rations were delivered twice a week and that meant not until tomorrow. I dare not repeat all the adjectives used between the inmates of our hut the next morning while applying icy water to our bodies under supervision of a most unfriendly Sergeant. Food did not arrive till lunch time and after an unsightly scramble I succeeded in grabbing a loaf of bread, one tin of sardines and a block of the dark chocolate. I was familiar with the latter ever since Lebanon because it required the teeth of a wolfhound to penetrate apart from causing constipation. That afternoon we were marched to the centre attraction of the camp, a large open square of beaten down earth. From an open lorry parked there all of us were issued with a French Private's uniforms. Material was thick and coarse and they came in two ill fitting sizes, large and small. A few sarcastic remarks did not please our guardian: 'What do you know about World War One, you young brats?! Just remember, no alterations are allowed until after the inspection.'

Few days went by and we were getting used to discomforts and hunger when the final deprivation reared its ugly head. Our Spanish predecessors had left behind a thriving colony of lice and from the general scratching and cursing it was obvious that no one was exempt. In desperation, we tried everything from boiling water to rolling an improvised pin across our shirts and underwear. All in vain . . . In fact, the nasty blood suckers kept us company throughout our ordeal in France. During the nightmarish 3 months in camp Septfont there was hardly any military training, certainly nothing to do with the war which, in any case, came to a grinding halt. No one thought it was necessary to introduce even one gun or a bullet to our motley selection of volunteers. I realised that my preoccupation with the daily survival blunted my sense of humour and worse still made me indifferent to previously cherished feelings towards my dear ones and even my country. But I did manage to learn some basic French, sharing one book of instruction with ten other fellows while the rest improved upon such skills as blackjack and poker, at the expense of few naive victims like myself and Vitold. These ill gotten gains enabled Jurek and Bolek to visit the provincial town of Montauban whereas our combined weekly pay would not be sufficient to cover cost of a single bus fare. Our pals returned with mouth watering tales of food, bistros and restaurants, lovely girls and sweet music, surprisingly enjoyed by a number of our own compatriots in smart uniforms. Jurek, who during his visit, feasted on one long roll and a piece of cheese was in no mood for tolerance.

'Doesn't it make you sick! We learned that one of those Corporals can afford a boarding house room nearly every weekend and can live like a lord.'

'And guess what,' added Bolek sadly, 'in compliance with the French Forces scales of pay our regular troops receive unbelievable salaries while the conscripts such as us suppose to rely on family support . . .' Here he hesitated to adopt a more pompous tone of voice, ' . . . to provide all the extras necessary to keep up with the civilised society.'

At this point I could not hold back my feelings any longer. 'What has this bloody place to do with civilisation or culture. Ever since I was a kid, and I am sure you heard the same rubbish time and time again, I was made to believe that the standard of living we Poles have to endure was puny in comparison with the sophisticated and luxurious life in the West. Now we know, France is not full of Pasteurs, Bizets, ballerinas or fashion models but where ever they are they are not using pissoirs like ours or scratch their arses all day.'

A dozen or so of fellows nearby who could not help overhearing my outburst joined in general condemnation of all authority, Polish and French. 'You're quite right, Jacek, we've been sold down the river. When they come next week, or whenever, we'll give them hell!'

'They' were, as rumours would have it, a group of examiners and recruiting officers whose arrival had been expected on several occasions before. Since, to date, it had not materialised no one, among our crowd of mainly school leavers, really believed in their existence.

However, when 'they' did arrive and interviews began even the most verbose barrack room lawyers kept their mouths shut hoping for a quick escape from the hell camp.

My interview, well rehearsed under Jurek's guidance, went surprisingly smoothly helped by a slight alteration to my identity card which added exactly one year to my date of birth and by the corroborating statement of my faithful, lying pals proving that I was member of the Air Cadet Force in Deblin. As a result I was accepted into the Polish Air Force as trainee aircrew and in company of three smiling rascals arrived in Le Bourget near Paris two weeks later to await training,

Unfortunately, April in Paris did not live up to its reputation as far as we were concerned. More comfort available in the newly constructed barrack blocks was still marred by the ever present lice and our daily activities had precious little to do with the aspiring aviators' ambitions. Boringly we were marched up and down the roads between the concrete blocks and attended a few French lessons. Hangars on the far side of the aerodrome were out of bounds and our eager eyes could only watch aircraft taking off and landing behind security fences. If there was any training going on it was kept a military secret from such as us. Instead, it was decided eventually to allow us an experience of doubtful value in aircraft spares production. We ended up doing night shifts in a converted Renault factory on the outskirts of the city, moving trolleys full of nuts and bolts from one end of assembly line to another. One bonus from my conversion to a labourer was a rapid progress in French and I was able to travel on Paris Metro using basic language in conversation with the natives. Alas, except for admiring the views and posters advertising gay Parisian life and many pleasures in this beautiful city, I was quite unable to sample any of them due to the persistent currency vacuum.

Back in the barracks a music system was blasting patriotic songs like: 'We're going to hang out washing on the Ziegfried line,' and time was uneventfully progressing towards May. There seemed complete lack of urgency around us as politicians continued to belittle Hitler's rantings and clearly defined ambitions in Mein Kampf while our military leaders appeared to have learned nothing from the blitzkrieg in Poland, doggedly trusting 'impenetrable' Maginot line. In retrospect, therefore, it should have been no surprise that Germany found this First World War concept inviting in 1940. Yet, myself, like the rest of my compatriots in the Le Bourget barracks could hardly believe our ears when on the 10th May, early in the morning, the BBC announced the enemy offensive and followed it with news of the panzer's daily progress through the Low Countries. Like in all the wartime bulletins there was still an air of optimism and half truths, peppered with quotations of unsustainable losses incurred by the invaders to the accompaniment of morale rousing music. All this, however, did not seem to deter the German tanks. Rapid advance split retreating Allied Forces through the middle and drove the British relentlessly towards Dunkirk and an eventual heroic evacuation. Arrival of June brought more disasters as the relentless panzers managed to outmanoeuvre French defences in an all out attack and within days smashed their way into the heart of France. By this time our unit which consisted of approximately 50 Poles was more then ready to move. Three Peugot lorries and two vans were 'rescued' from the airfield and each one of us was allocated a vehicle in advance. Our few remaining French guardians, panicked by the news of a German armoured column moving steadily from the north-west to within 30 kilometers of Paris, did not seem to mind. As we loaded our vehicles the French radio announced the commencement of surrender negotiations with the Germans. There was only one way out. Guided by experts of evasion from last September's campaign, in the shape of two Cavalry Officers, our tiny convoy headed south-west towards Le Mans, Rennes and eventually port of St Malo, the nearest route to Channel Isles and hopefully England. Along these highways we saw the effect of sudden collapse of another country as well as that of a powerful alliance, after propaganda instilled overconfidence and patriotic enthusiasm terminated in shock and fear. There was scarcely a human being in sight and those still out in the streets of towns and villages disappeared indoors at the first sight of our leading vehicle. The most significant witness to a breakdown of morale in the retreating armies was the amassment of abandoned military gear lying in the ditches by the roadside. Apart from uniforms and helmets, discarded transport such as ammunition trailers and bowsers, poked out sadly from under torn camouflage netting strung between the poplars lining endless straight roads. Lucky for us, one of those fuel tanks proved most useful a few days later in our ambitious escape attempt.

After a long, sweaty and thirsty journey, St Malo proved another disappointment. Every house was firmly locked, citizens hiding away as if expecting a plague, no boats in the harbour, and no food or water. Prolonged knocking on several doors of the port offices produced a frightened face of an old caretaker who asked in a shaky voice if we knew the war was over. 'Well, not for us, Monsieur,' says one of our leaders as he rams his foot firmly in the door. Unable to lock himself in again the Frenchman waved his hands in desperation and pleaded. 'Please go, la guerre finis, you're in uniform . . . if the Bosh sees you here he will come and bomb us.'

'Don't worry, old son, we are not here for a holiday, just tell us where the boats are and we are off'

'I swear, I do not know, Monsieur, all have been taken last week by our fishermen, could be Jersey, could be Brest.'

'Any fresh water or food nearby?'

Again his answer was negative but he did point to a long sandy beach on the west side of the bay. 'There are some facilities for tourists there, but please go as soon as you can.'

It took only half an hour to get to the seaside holiday resort of Dinard, a name advertised on many road signposts out of St Malo. Sun was now low on the horizon and once again no one in sight. It was decided therefore to settle between a few deserted chalets amongst sandy dunes and rhododendron shrubs in full blossom. Such completely unexpected turn of events resulted in a general outburst of fun and badly needed relaxation as we dashed for the sea in an orgy of juvenile tomfoolery and laughter. I spend that warm June night with my friends under the starry sky, tucked away in the soft sand, wondering why the world is so ugly when it could be so beautiful. Self pity kept nagging my soul after only a brief taste of pleasures which managed to avoid me and my generation for what seemed like an eternity. To the pacifying sound of gently lapping sea nearby we shared our thoughts and talked about the care free days back home until silenced by fatigue and badly needed sleep.

Early next morning I woke up to the sound of usual scratching and moaning of my comrades some of whom were already finishing breakfast of remaining stale bread and fresh water which was still running from the beach showers after yesterday's frolics. Soon, a small party was organised to investigate any possibility of evacuation, whereabouts of Germans and, of course, sources of food and petrol. While they disappeared into the mainland everyone took a refreshing dip in the sea, grateful for a chance to cool off in ever rising heat of the day and anxiously awaited the news. We were obviously ready to go at the shortest of notices but proximity of freedom in the shape of the English coast which one could almost smell across the Channel, was so inviting no one was ready to

consider running away from it. Just after midday our Captain's van
with his reconnaissance party arrived back in a cloud of dust and
were immediately surrounded by anxious faces and multitude of
questions. Apparently, Germans have not made much progress
westwards knowing that they can do it any time later and instead
concentrated on the huge propaganda exercise of humiliating France
by parading panzers past the Arc de Triomphe. We soon learned that
it was impossible even to talk to once proud people about the war or
continuation of it, especially to the tear shedding women and a few
old citizens left behind in Dinard but money, always being useful,
managed to persuade them to part with freshly baked bread, smoked
pork and cheese. Day later, with all hopes of evacuation by sea
gone, a decision was made to abandon our temporary Shangri-La
and head for the Spanish border. To join the main south bound
route from St Malo one had to back-pedal via Rennes and our
initial problem was acquisition of fuel. Everyone hoped that the
abandoned bowser which we saw on our way here was still resting
in the ditch few kilometers from city's outskirts. The small tanker
was indeed still in the same spot seemingly forgotten in panic
withdrawal of French troops. While for days no one else showed
any interest in its contents our enthusiastic experts managed to
empty most of it in less than an hour filling up all vehicles and
every spare can. One major chunk of good fortune behind us still
left ahead an awsome challenge and some serious thoughts for
consideration: the distance of more than 600 kilometers through
chaos stricken and demoralised country to reach our chancy haven
with no alternative in sight. At this stage no one suffered from
excess of optimism but the decision was made and all of us were
determined to succeed.

In formation of one truck up front, lorries in the middle and
second truck behind we motored steadily through the almost empty
streets of Rennes, unlikely situation for crossroads of Brittany as
well as a major railway junction. Our route took us eventually close
to the vast railway yards when the lead vehicle waved us down to a
halt. It was midday and we were glad to stretch our legs.

'Five minutes for a cigarette and a leak,' barked the driver.

On our right, below an embankment, spread endless assortment of motionless wagons many with doors wide open and long flat trolleys loaded with bulging wine casks.

'Hey, Sarge, take a look at all the goodies down there. How about a quick recce?' suggests Jurek.

'Don't be silly, we haven't got time.'

'We haven't got many rations left either. It won't hurt to ask the Captain, there isn't a soul in sight.'

Encouraged now by the rest of us our Sergeant walked up forward to the lead vehicle and returned a minute later with a self satisfied appearance of authority. 'I want six volunteers with flasks and a couple of kit bags to go down there and see if there is anything worth while bringing back.'

Everyone stepped forward. 'Me Sarge, and me, and me . . .'

'Hold it, hold it! I said only six, that means you,' he looked at Jurek, 'and these five next to you. You have 15 minutes without causing any damage or upsetting gendarmes.'

We watched them sneak in and out between the wagons until they disappeared round the bend of rail tracks.

First two to climb the embankment on return heaved under the weight of kitbags full of potatoes, Jurek and Bolek arrived with at least a dozen flasks each strung together across their shoulders, followed by the remaining two, labouring up hill with an enormous round cheese wrapped in layers of muslin. No one really knew what kind of fromage it was but despite sarcasm and indigestible suggestions we were greatly relieved that the smell which arrived with it came from the sweat sodden shirts of the carriers and not the cheese. Few minutes later we were back on the road heading this time for Nantes. Rocking in the discomfort of hard bench seats, exhaust smell and hot air swirling under the flapping canvas, it did not take very long for my inventive companions to rise above our temporary problems.

'How much wine have we salvaged in this truck?' says one.

'I have four cans here,' Bolek points below his seat, 'that's all Sarge would allow per wagon.'

'Well there are only ten of us, that should be enough.'

I interrupted the laughter. 'You're not going to drink it now, in this heat? Save it for the supper, it could be your last one.' My experience of coarse red wine made me shudder at the thought of being ill again and I did not want to expose this weakness to my hardened mates.

'Just listen to this prophet,' Jurek seemed to have guessed my motives, 'he doesn't smoke either, mammie's boy, come on, one sip won't hurt you.'

He passed me the opened flask and I pretended to take a large gulp without screwing my face in distaste. 'This stuff is better than that last lot you gave me in Lebanon,' I lied.

It was just as well that engine noise drowned the ensuing joviality and loud voices but lack of reaction from the cab up front made me think that our Sarge had also sampled his share of spoils. Hours later, I watched different scene of tired sleepy bodies trying to keep company with their seats while the convoy continued past Nantes and La Rochelle. Our military vehicles and French uniforms did not raise any eyebrows as we drove through towns, villages and acres of famous vinyards and the local gendarmes, one could see again here and there, helped even with directions on two occasions. Things were going well, we thought, until some 50 kilometers from Bordeaux when our lorry swerved from side to side, finally grinding to a sudden halt at a peculiar angle and throwing us all forward in a heap. We scrambled out with just a few scratches and bruises to find out that after a tyre burst the vehicle skidded into the roadside ditch ripping its steering rods apart. Even with the assistance of all other drivers nothing could be done and twelve of us and the stores had to transfer to the three remaining trucks. With only an hour of daylight left it was decided to spend the night few hundred meters further on, just off the highway and out of sight of passing traffic.

It was a tired and subdued company that has settled for the night after a very basic supper and for the first time since its acquisition no one joked about smelly French cheese shared out and eaten that evening. Unable to settle on the hard ground I began to search desperately for a realistic solution to my predicament: what did happen to those ideals and romantic notions of last year, life is much more complicated than you ever imagined . . . who would have thought that you would lose two wars within nine months after such grand expectations and trust in your allies. Still, with your experience and at the age of eighteen you had to trust somebody . . . now you are heading for another internment even though your military contribution apart from Warsaw amounts to nothing and you have not fired a shot in anger. At least one hope remains, as long as my three pals, Jurek, Vitold and Bolek, keep me company . . . like the three legendary musketeers they seem to find a way out of any tight corner . . .

I woke up, daylight barely showing, to the sounds of packing and Jurek's voice telling somebody not to forget the potatoes. Stiff, cold and hungry I clambered into the last lorry squeezing tight between my pals. Including two drivers up front there were now 20 of us in this wagon and things were not getting any more comfortable as we heaved across the roadside ditch and away towards Bordeaux. Vitold who was sitting next to me began to study his pocket calendar.

'You won't believe it,' he muttered, 'It's already 17th June, wouldn't it be nice to know what the hell is happening behind our backs now. Maybe the Gerry is already ahead of us.'

'I couldn't care less at this time,' I retorted, 'whatever is ahead it will not make us any happier. Let's hope though that Frenchies are still talking to them and no one has sold us down the river before we reach Pyrenees.'

'You're right,' agreed Bolek, 'on the other side Franco is not waiting to greet us with open arms either, his neutrality is 100 per cent pro Hitler.'

This air of resignation began to affect all of us and lasted until we approached the outskirts of Bordeaux when amid sound of brakes our convoy came to another unscheduled halt destroying all conversation. Few fellows at the rear managed to stretch their heads above the canvas roof. 'Well I'll be damned,' says one in a subdued voice, 'we are surrounded by gendarmes and that's all we need.' In fact, we were stopped by smart regulars of French Army guarding one of the bridges across river Garonne who were not quite satisfied with either our identity or our presence so far from the battlefields. After some arguments and a lot of hand waving up forward they escorted our complete convoy away from the intended route to a huge depot of war leftovers where we were parked between man made earth embankment and rows of immobilised vehicles and instructed to await further orders. After an hour, which seemed like an eternity, two French officers arrived and without getting out of the car summoned our leaders to what appeared a lengthy conference while the rest of us stood by the vehicles anxiously awaiting news. It was already midday when they departed and we learned that the newly formed French government has already signed peace treaty with the Germans, part of which included immediate withdrawal of all French troops and demilitarisation of all areas outside the designated part south of Massif Central. Therefore, our Polish military unit must cease to exist, vehicles and arms must be left here, but we do have a choice of moving down south with the other disbanded troops.

'Bloody cheek! What a let down! War may have finished for the Frogs but not for us, right fellows?' rang out the chorus of stubborn defiance. Soon, however, things calmed down when it became obvious that more than shouting and banner waving was required to get us out of this sorry mess. Unopposed, Germans have already reached the Atlantic coast occupying towns and harbours including Brest, Lorient and St Nazaire. Our original plan of sticking close to the Bay of Biscay coastline until Spanish border seemed still the best way out. We had less than 200 kilometers to go but now we had to outwit the French as well. There was no question therefore of handing over our vehicles and it was decided to split our convoy into individual units and remove all Polish military insignia, hoping also that no more road blocks existed between Bordeaux and Biarritz, last big town before Spain.

We waited, fingers crossed, until the few remaining French soldiers disappeared between the rows of immobilised vehicles, probably looking for vacant spaces to fill with our lot. On a given signal all of us jumped back into the trucks and lorries and with minimum engine noise we drove slowly out of the compound without causing anyone's surprise. Accelerating towards the built up area we soon parted company with all military installations and were glad to find some tall roadside shrubbery where it was possible to shelter and enable us to split up the convoy into separate vehicles at five minute intervals. Now on our own, Jurek and I moved into the driver's cab to help with navigation and in my case with any French that maybe required. The rest stayed hidden under the canvas in the back as instructed. Unlike the other towns we drove through since Paris Bordeaux streets were packed with cars, bicycles and pedestrians while shops opened for business gave an appearance of normality. Obviously no one expected the war to reach this far and most fortunately for us all the road signs were left in place. By late afternoon we found ourselves making steady progress on an open road to Biarritz but keeping an anxious watch on our fuel state with just over 150 kilometers to go. The lads in the back, freed now from the heat under the canvas, became more vociferous pointing out that no one has eaten since the day before and it was time to do something about it. We were now motoring through a wooded countryside and the pangs of hunger prompted us eventually to stop in a small clearing amongst the pines. This time nobody protested about one course meal of baked potatoes, the only food left in our lorry, but by the time the last of them were picked out of the ashes of two fires it was dark again. We decided to leave the final assault on Spain till next day .

Despite warmth throughout the night another slumber on the hard ground did not improve condition of stiff and aching limbs and a few uncomplimentary groans accompanied our crew as we climbed back on board the 3-tonner before sunrise. The last 20 litre can of petrol was already emptied into main tank and we were ready for off once again. Unmolested, we travelled through Bayonne and Biarritz without seeing a soul in uniform until later that morning when we reached the approaches to St Jean de Luz only one kilometer from the Spanish border. This small coastal town turned out to be quite a surprise.

As far as one could see to our right the Biscay Bay coastline stretched eastwards and with a few palms close to the sea, an endless sandy beach appeared more like a desert island than the European coast. Soon we found ourselves between two rows of parked vehicles, mostly of military variety, until first dwellings came in view where abandoned lorries made further progress impossible. Ahead, a large crowd filled the main street and the sound of many voices filled the air between the tightly packed houses. It was time to abandon our truck as well and find out what the hell was going on. Sticking close together we made our way into the crowd of dirty, unshaven men who, like ourselves, were dressed in dust covered French uniforms and spoke our language. Where all of them came from was not immediately important to us but the reason for their gathering here was.

'See that ship on the horizon?' one of them points towards the sea, 'the rumour has it she is British, ready to evacuate their consular staff from southern France.'

I stood on my toes with the rest of our company in an attempt to locate the ship, looking over the heads of men in front while he continued: 'Haven't you heard? Frenchies have a new government in what they call Vichy France, bloody collaborators. Brits don't like it anymore than we do and broke off all diplomatic relations with this lot.'

'So what has it got to do with us?'

'There is a chance, they say, that we might be evacuated too.'

At that moment of time it was hard to believe that any such thing could happen, particularly after so many let downs, but a drowning man, it is said, will grab a razor-blade to save himself and we decided to wait with the rest and see what happens.

The ship was there all right and her name was Arrandora Star. In the afternoon a launch appeared off the beach and everyone, except the inhabitants of St Jean de Luz, rushed to meet the sailors. Led by a very young Subaltern in naval uniform, armed with a Thompson machine gun, a party of six Marines, also armed, made their way past the crowd of well-wishers straight for the two large wooden storage buildings near a jetty opposite. Situation similar to that in St Malo developed with inhabitants hiding behind bolted doors and trying to ignore all the noise and hassle outside. Not being able to understand more than a dozen words of English between all of us it was nothing but guess work what the Navy was after. Having failed to arouse a soul on the sea front, they marched smartly into the town still followed by a curious crowd and finally halted outside the portals of an important looking residence. Above the large double doors, carved in stone were letters: GENDARMERIE. Few loud bangs on the knocker had no effect on the occupants at first but a well directed hit with a rifle butt on the lock itself did. The door flung open and revealed two frightened, unshaven individuals, arms up in the air, apologising for the delay. Although I was some 20

*Off St Jean de Luz, 1940. Arrandora Star
evacuating remains of escaping troops*

meters from the action I heard the young officer speak in short, sharp terms, his French far from perfect.

'Put your arms down. Who is in charge here?'

'Monsieur le Maire.'

'Where is he?'

'He is ill in bed . . . in his house . . .'

'Where is that?!'

'Next door, over there, Monsieur.'

Frustration was beginning to show on Marine's face. 'Fetch him,' he snapped, 'fetch him now!' He slapped his Thompson with one hand as the petrified Frenchmen side stepped past him with obvious relief of being released from further conversation. Two of the armed sailors escorted our reluctant messengers past the crowd outside keeping close eye on their charges.

The beret of Monsieur le Maire, tall stooping figure of a man, appeared few minutes later as he entered the entrance hall where the Sublieutenant waited by the opened doors. This time the conversation was much more subdued but we did see a large wad of bank notes

51

being handed over to the Frenchman with one hand while the other still leaned on the machine gun. The injection of cash resulted in an instant recovery of Monsieur le Maire and he walked out sprightly, no longer stooping, in the direction of fishing smacks tied up by the jetty. Meanwhile three Polish officers remained in conference with the Marine. They emerged few minutes later trying vainly to conceal broad grins on their faces and confirmed that that we are going to England after all. The roar that followed must have been heard in Spain. I remember one Major appealing for silence and civilised behaviour in front of our British allies while instructions were given to divide the multitude into groups of no more than twenty men each, all to assemble on the beach in orderly fashion and await further orders.

Myself and my three mates managed again to stick together as we watched French fishermen man their boats, fill them to capacity with men ahead of us and depart into the open sea accompanied by noisy staccato of the diesels.

I was more than impressed. 'So that's what the money was for! Have you ever seen such leadership and discipline before? How could seven smart sailors resolve this situation in a matter of hours is unbelievable. Good old British Navy!'

'It makes you wonder if we have joined the right Service,' added Vitold.

We boarded our fishing boat late that afternoon and made the one mile passage to Arrandora Star in shallow, calm for a change waters of Biscay Bay. My amazement at the scale of the whole operation grew as I stepped onto the top deck of this rather ancient merchantman with hardly a space to swing a cat. With humans packed like sardines the boats continued to shuttle until there was not an inch of space left on the lower decks either. Not a word of complaint, no sensation of hunger or discomfort, just a mass of satisfied customers.

As the sun approached the end of its daily journey rattle of the anchor chain from the bows coincided with the departure of the last Frenchman and with a billowing trail of black smoke behind her Arrandora Star headed for the Atlantic.

CHAPTER 4

Learning Fast

My first introduction to England was a cup of tea. Actually, it was just a tin mug served from a big urn on the lower deck where an endless queue of starving men awaited their first meal for days. One packet of biscuits per head completed the feast and it became apparent that with well over a thousand unexpected passengers strict rationing was essential. However, tiredness came to the rescue on the first night at sea and every deck and passage of Arrandora Star soon reverberated with the sounds of heavy breathing and sporadic snoring. Our unprotected vessel, so close to the enemy, wisely chose to put the greatest distance between us and the occupied coastline as quickly as possible for in the morning there was no sign of land. During the next four days everyone's involvement in the proceedings concentrated on a search for periscopes after some scaremongers suggested that we made a perfect target for U-boats and no one could understand why it took such a long time to reach our destination. Eventually, on 23rd June, we entered the Irish Sea from the north, having circumnavigated Ireland's Atlantic shores. Then, I caught my first glimpse of England.

In perfect visibility one could distinguish clusters of red brick houses against the deep green background of rising hills long before the ship entered Merseyside Bay. Soaking up the unexpected and fascinating views of Liverpool's forefront I hardly noticed the huge gateway to the docks slowly passing by as the Arrandora Star made slow but dignified way towards her mooring. There, to everyone's surprise, a sizable crowd of mainly dock workers appeared, even before the warps were cast ashore, waving and cheering in the first real welcome I had experienced since leaving Poland. Crammed against the ship's rails we waved back with genuine enthusiasm until ordered to move down for disembarkation. The large area of concrete in front of the storage sheds soon became a mass of rocking men, unsteady on their legs after four days at sea, but faces full of beaming smiles. Despite of our pitiful condition, dirty clothing and smelly bodies a few young girls clad in overalls rushed the barriers with kisses and even bars of chocolate on offer. The only bewilderment occurred when three old men armed with wooden spikes, not unlike broom handles and carrying the words 'Home Guard' on their arm bands arrived to chaperon the young females out of the compound. 'I hope they are not waiting for German paratroopers,' said someone to our amusement but later when the field kitchens arrived with the first square meal for weeks I am sure everyone thought that they had arrived in paradise.

Once again we were herded into buses and arrived at a railway station to meet a waiting train which consisted of a dozen or more coaches split into many compartments but with no sign of corridors. I discovered later that they were mainly used over short distances by workers and their families from inland industrial towns commuting to seaside resorts on public holidays. One thing for certain, they were capable of packing in hundreds of passengers, all seated, and that is how we arrived one and a half hour later on a railway siding few hundred yards from the entrance to the Royal Air Force Station Weeton in Lancashire. After Rumania, Lebanon and France my first impression of England was of cleanliness and neatness. Even though Weeton consisted mainly of Nissen huts and had no airfield, everything smelled of freshness. Tarmaced roads were spotless and lush green grass was cut to perfection. No one had to be ordered to enter the ablutions between the huts where showers and modern toilets were conspicuous by the absence of the foul smells we had become used to in France. Within 48 hours we were all deloused, our French uniforms removed and burned, proudly sporting the rather ill fitting uniforms of RAF wartime airmen. Such luxuries as jam for breakfast, tinned pineapple and other tropical fruit after each main meal were devoured with a keen eye on any leftovers. Witold and I managed to be accommodated in the same hut and, although Jurek and Bolek slept few doors away, we all met routinely at various chores and meal times.

'This is what I call service,' says Jurek patting his stomach after another dinner, 'but how long can it last?'

'Do you really care?' I tried a bit of realism, 'I am sure they are not fattening us up here just to keep this place clean and do few guard duties. Sooner or later another selection committee will have a go at us, you wait.'

'You're probably right, Jacek, but all these regulars from Lyon will have to go before anybody decides what to do with us, after all, they were the backbone of our Air Force in France, apart from the aircrew who flew out before the Gerries took over.'

'They are not only well trained,' butted in Bolek, 'but could they run! How did they get to St Jean de Luz before us, tell me. That must have been a sharp decision seeing how far behind us they were in the first place.'

There and then we all agreed that as microbes in the action so far in this war we had a mighty long way to go before we could be of any use.

During the following two months I began to study yet another language and spent many hours trying to memorise the vagaries of the English spelling and pronunciation. Most of the encouragement as far as I was concerned came from the comparably poor progress of my companions, who discovered early the meaning of 'clever dick' and used it often when seeking my help in translation. Also, our pay of 2 shillings a day enabled us to visit the famous seaside resort of Blackpool with its impressive attractions such as the Pleasure Beach skating rink. Invaluable help in conversation came from dozens of pretty girls gliding on ice each Saturday, ready to help young Polish heroes while showing off their colourful, shorter than short skirts. This innocent relationship fascinated us every bit as much as the girls, whose only experience of foreigners so far came from the cinema. Little did I know at that time that much later I would marry one of them. As well as the females each Pole was openly welcomed by general public of all ages, probably impressed by their good manners or accents never heard before and whose patriotism and defiance was equal to both sides. However, having lost two wars long before my 19th birthday I could not help sharing the private view of my compatriots that the desperate reality of Germany's might, only 18 miles across the Channel, has not yet dawned on the majority of our hosts.

Warm and sunny, August arrived still without any military activity on land but at sea menacing U-boats began to inflict serious losses on merchant shipping and everyone in Weeton was particularly sad to hear that the Arrandora Star was sunk on the way to Canada with heavy loss of life. In Britain everyone was now preparing for the imminent invasion without a hint of panic but with much determination instilled through radio and the press by a bulldog of a man called Winston Churchill. It was then that myself and my friends became aware that our selection to aircrew in France was still valid, subject to medical examination. We were granted the rank of ACH, an abbreviation of Aircraft Hand. A grand title which was accorded to all trainees about to take to air for the first time. It also meant sixpence a day more on pay parades. Sadly, within days, I parted company with my escape partners with promises of everlasting friendship, all posted to different flying stations but hoping to be reunited later.

I arrived in Northolt on the outskirts of London just in time to witness the first German bombing raids on that city. Here we go again, I thought, it worked in Warsaw and Rotterdam why not try it once more! If you are a German you must be systematic. There was, however, one basic difference, as I soon discovered.

In the virtual non stop roar of Spitfires scrambling from all directions no one paid the slightest attention to my arrival outside a dispersal hut of 303 Polish fighter squadron where I stood mesmerised, mouth wide open, watching the spectacular scene around me. I would have been there rooted to the spot till next day if it was not for two pilots walking away from their aircraft, leather helmets slung across their Mae Wests, busily gesticulating while excited voices, in the half Polish and half English aircrew jargon, rang victory bells. Obviously unaccustomed to things standing still, one of them bumped into my shoulder and stopped in his tracks.

'Have you nothing better to do? Get moving and I take two sugars in my coffee, szybko!'

Before I could even open my mouth they turned away and entered the hut. Bemused, I decided to follow. The long corrugated iron hut was divided in two, one half being a pilot's rest room and on the door of partition between the two, a large notice read: BRIEFING ONLY. Three officers and one Sergeant, all in flying kit, were spread out now in easy chairs still explaining to each other how one Heinkel and one Messerschmitt will never darken blue skies again and I did not dare interrupt. I made my way towards the nearest corner of the room away from the conversation and waited for something to happen. The pilot who outside had outmaneuvred the enemy aircraft with a hand before it struck my arm suddenly remembered his order.

'I'll be blown, one could die of thirst here.' He turned to me. 'Can't you see the kettle over there,' he pointed to a table behind him, 'haven't you been here before, son?'

'No sir, I have only just arrived on the station from Weeton.'

'Weeton? Where the hell is that?'

'It's a holding station in Lancashire, sir.'

'So what did they send you here for?'

'I don't know really,' they all burst out laughing as I quickly corrected myself, 'I am supposed to get some aircraft experience while waiting for pilot training.'

'Oh, that's different, what is your name?'

'Blocki, sir.'

'Well Blocki, get behind that kettle and seeing what a bright lad you are, we'll have four coffees this time!'

My enthusiasm undaunted I served drinks to the heroes of the Battle of Britain for two weeks before being promoted to the heart pulsating experience of standing on a Spitfire wing and helping the pilots to strap in before scrambles or helping to carry their parachutes after landing. During that time I began to appreciate the unquestioned comradeship between them and the rather fatalistic sense of humour they shared in moments of tension as well as in brief periods of relaxation. Only the tireless ground crews showed some emotion when two of our aircraft failed to return from a dog fight early in September and, in the tradition of the squadron, everyone who paraded next day was presented with a drink, aptly named Messerschmitt. It consisted of equal measures of whisky, vodka and rum and was drunk in one gulp in memory of the two pilots. I was ill for two days and apologised profusely afterwards. Despite the sacrifices and sweat I witnessed during those weeks in Northolt, it never occurred to me or any one I met there that one day this heroic battle would be recognised as the turning point of the war.

By the end of September German losses forced them to abandon their daylight raids, and, unknown to the rest of the world then, any plans they had for the invasion of England. At last our fighter squadrons tasted a well deserved break from the maximum operational effort while concentrating on often neglected maintenance and routine administration. On the grassy dispersal hard working fitters now allowed me to clean engine cowlings and even sit inside a Spitfire cockpit, thrilling at the thought of a real flight. Just as I was getting to know everyone on the squadron, I was called in front of the Adjutant who told me I was posted back to Weeton. I found that quite heart breaking at first but the bitter pill was sweetened a day later when written posting orders arrived instructing me to report first to the Aircrew Medical Board in St John's Wood, London, which meant another step nearer flying.

I arrived there on a wet October morning after a prolonged search in a large building complex of pre-war apartments. I was told to join the queue of twenty or more young airmen of various ranks stretching down the corridor outside. After half an hour of listening to a few 'experts', some of whom had failed the medical once before, I realised that this would be no walk over and soon lost my confidence. Having never experienced such a microscopic examination before, I began to believe that it takes a super human being to outwit the doctors who insist on you blowing a column of mercury to the height of three feet and then hold your breath for at least 60 seconds as one of the tricks necessary to become a pilot. 'You must be joking,' I said to an English lad who apparently had to come back after getting rid of a cold. But, to my horror, he was not. This mercury trick followed eyesight, hearing and reflexes checks. Since I preferred to die rather than fail, my face, after a minute without breathing, changed colour to a ripe beetroot. For many years afterwards I tried to find out what this test really proved but examining doctors of the Royal Air Force were determined to keep it an official secret. The best news came after a three times repeated heartbeat count from a disbelieving doctor, who eventually congratulated me on the slowest heart he had ever listened to in a living person and smiled for the first time since I entered his office. 'There is nothing wrong with you, son,' he declared.

Rather big headed I arrived back in Weeton only to be told to report to the Polish Headquarters in Blackpool. Accommodated in one of the many boarding houses behind the 6 mile long Promenade I was delighted to find Jurek and Witold next door who had already started a thriving ground school for future aviators. As well as parading every morning with thousands of recruits of various trades, our Polish section had at least two hours a day of English lessons in between subjects like Morse and aircraft recognition. Such night life as playing poker or watching the girls go by was soon rudely interrupted by the first German night raid on Liverpool and after that we spent much of the 1941 winter on the roofs of tall buildings, told to look out for bombs and fires, thus freeing the local Home Guard to man the piers in case of an invasion from the sea. Most of the light hearted attitude, however, soon dissipated at the news from elsewhere in Britain. Night after night, the shocking and gruesome destruction of cities and massive killing of the civilian population created not only anger but united the whole of the people in a determined effort to react with equal force. Needless to say, myself and all my young companions were beginning to itch more for a fight with every passing day.

First to go was Jurek. Witold and I then departed after what seemed an endless wait of two months. Our destination: No15 EFTS (Elementary Flying Training School), Carlisle. What joy, yet a moment of truth! The grass airfield of Kingston, with two blister hangars and prefab offices in-between, seemed like heaven after the classrooms and concrete parade grounds of Blackpool. The non-stop buzz of Magisters taking off and landing filled me with instant excitement and a sense of nervous anticipation. Our course of twelve young fellows, myself being the youngest, was allocated in groups of three to various instructors and, after the initial briefing by the Commanding Officer, I was introduced to Sgt. Pilot Pullman who was to shape my future for the next 10 weeks and first 50 flying hours. He was one of the many pre-war non commissioned officers who came into the RAF as reservists under a title of Sprog (Sergeant Pilot Recruited On Gratuity) and whose experience proved more than useful in the early days of the war. At first I found his broad Scottish accent a bit of a handicap but I soon discovered that there were other means of communication available to him. From the back cockpit of the Magister he wielded the aircraft control locking stick like a weapon whenever the poor unfortunate in the front seat mis-understood him. Not a great man in stature but his god-like authority was never questioned by students who bounced the aircraft more than once on landing. I am no more likely to forget his favourite pearl of wisdom: 'You bloody Poles don't understand anything. The hardest thing about flying is the ground!', than the sensation of first ever flight. In this the feel of controls, the ever louder drone of engine in front, charge of air past an open cockpit and finally effortless lift off above the rushing ground beneath was exhilarating. I made my first solo, within the strictly prescribed 5 hours after Flight Commander's check, with only 5 minutes to spare and realised that telling lies about my previous experience on the selection board was not a very wise thing. With a well concealed sympathy for human nature, Sgt. Pullman listened to the truth and expressed himself in his usual manner. 'How can you trust anybody?!' He paused, then looked around if anyone was listening. 'It's a bonny mess, you stupid lad, but since you did make first solo I'll see if I can improve your brain without getting you and me court marshalled.'

This he did with some success and after two weeks of extra attention the three dimensional reactions fell in place. I passed the course with an average assessment and like the rest of eleven students stated as my choice for future flying: Fighter Command. Now, either someone lost our preference for posting forms or chose to ignore them for Service reasons but, before we were sent on a week's leave, the CO told us we were all going to South Cerney to fly Oxfords. Those who had carried pictures of a Spitfire before their eyes for weeks nearly cried that day. I also could not see myself flying multi-engined aircraft but Sgt. Pullman who reckoned I was too slow to catch cold said to me that he did not want to see German fighters notch up an easy kill and I must not complain at this stage.

55 Course – South Cerney, Oxfordshire, 1941

The summer of 1941 was still in full swing when I entered the portals of RAF South Cerney, home of No 3 SFTS (Secondary Flying Training School). Still with a rank of LAC Pilot, my pay reached 3 pounds a week and life was getting much more comfortable while a permanent barrack block offered almost luxurious accommodation in comparison with the past. The NAAFI Club provided recreation such as snooker, darts and music, while drinks and snacks were available at ridiculous prices. All that, after recent deprivations, was greatly appreciated.

The twin engined Airspeed Oxford was not an easy trainer to fly yet I found no difficulty in tackling the course which included my first night flying. Some of the others did not fare too well, three having failed to pass and, in one stupid accident, our comrade who so dearly wanted to fly a Spitfire killed himself trying unauthorised low level aerobatics. This incident more than anything acted as a cold shower on the rest and since I would not even dream of tearing round the sky like that in the first place, proved that Sgt. Pullman was not a bad judge of human character and ability. Three months after Carlisle I passed out on Oxfords having added 75 flying hours to my log book's total and early in December arrived in Bramcote with brand new chevrons of a sergeant.

Here in the Midlands was one of those meeting places of future Bomber Command crews guided by selectors of 18 OTU (Operational Training Unit). The whole place was like a huge beehive, full of recently qualified pilots, navigators, wireless operators, air gunners and bomb-aimers and I anxiously awaited that momentous encounter from the day I arrived there. The ground school, however, terminating in examination in subjects such as astro navigation, meteorology and signals, had to come first and did not allow me much time to dwell on the uncertainties of the future.

Christmas of 1941, like my 20th birthday, passed almost unnoticed and it was not until the following March that I ceased to be a bookworm and returned to flying. At first the pilot's conversion to a Wellington kept me in the permanently busy circuit of the airfield and despite of my initial doubts, after coming face to face with this comparatively enormous machine, flying it was surprisingly trouble free. Various instructors and crews followed at this stage until I was considered fit to fly solo on a few exercises in the local area. After landing from one of those trips I entered the crew room and found everyone in it staring and gesticulating in front of the notice board. That was the day when the names of Prot, the navigator, Henryk, wireless operator, Stefan, bomb-aimer and two gunners, Kazik and Piotr appeared next to mine forming one of the crews selected to continue further training together. Apart from Prot who was a pre-war trained Flying Officer we were all Sergeants and the first meeting of strangers was a little like a Board of Inquiry to find out who is who and why. I could not help noticing a hint of disappointment on Prot's face who eyed me from top to bottom, probably in disbelief that anyone looking like a schoolboy was going to be responsible for his safety. There was nothing to be done, however, about the most strict selection orders in force and nothing was said. This attitude of caution and awareness of the task ahead became apparent throughout Bramcote aircrew, after a series of fatal accidents, the most depressing of which resulted in the instant death of eight students and instructors after a fully laden Wellington with fuel and practice bombs hit a concrete bunker on take off and exploded less than 200 yards from our barrack block.

Half way through my course I was told to look after a family who arrived from Blackpool, invited in the usual way by the Station, after their friend and my pal Wladek and his crew were killed in a crash over the Scottish mountains. In this sad situation I met my future father-in-law, Jim Nadin, his wife Alice and to my surprise and great pleasure one of their daughters, Hilda, an eighteen year old honey blond whose film star appearance made me almost speechless in such demanding circumstances. The surprise element of our meeting came with realisation that she was one of the beauties I had admired on the ice rink nearly a year ago and she remembered it well. Before they left I had to promise to visit them in Blackpool at the first opportunity.

Alas, that promise had to wait for a long time despite occasional reminders from the most generous Jim. This was the time for serious concentration while the first lessons of survival imprinted themselves on our inexperienced minds. Several night cross-countries, invariably culminating in practice bombings on the many ranges from the Wash to the Scottish Isles, greatly contributed to our mutual confidence and began to create a sense of belonging and loyalty so characteristic of Bomber Command crews. Of course, the world events such as Japanese raid on Pearl Harbour or Germany's attack on Russia did not go unnoticed during my fledgling days in England. I do not think there was a Pole who believed that the sudden friendship between Hitler and Stalin, which carved up their country, would last and that bloody episode was met with more than hopeful satisfaction. But subsequent discovery by the Germans of the mass grave in Katyn of more than 5000 Polish officers, judiciary and policemen, all shot in the back of the head with a single bullet brought me to the point of despair. Even more depressing was the cowardly silence of Allied politicians in face of such a crime against humanity, as shaking hands with Stalin and his KGB officials continued. Bitter and twisted I said to my equally angry compatriots gathered by the radio: 'You just wait . . . one day the whole world will pay dearly for this.' Still, Germany remained a primary objective and, as time went by, everyone calmed down in a helpless situation.

When, at the end of May, we were finally told of our posting to 305 Polish Bomber Squadron in Lindholme, south Yorkshire, there was just one thought left: flying. Only six crews completed the full course, including Vitold's. All were dispersed between the other three Polish bomber squadrons, 300, 301 and 304 but not before the Sergeants Mess at Bramcote was emptied of beer.

I arrived in Lindholme on my own, the rest of the crew taking an opportunity of a few day's leave to seek the pleasures of big cities, especially girl friends, pursuit of which was surprisingly easy for aircrew with brand new wings on their battle tunics. According to Henryk, patriotism and money concocted a most effective aphrodisiac but, as I soon discovered, most of my friend's tales of romantic achievements were built on hope rather than reality. My own tendency to enjoy the good life of an easy chair, clean sheets and three square meals a day, as long as they lasted, enabled me to avoid walking the streets in pouring rain for a few minutes of conversation with a strange female. From the first day I spent on this bomber station, however, I realised how different life will be from any notions I may have had about my new squadron.

I reported to the Station Headquarters, as instructed. My presence duly recorded by the administrators, I was then pointed in the direction of a huge hangar, home of 305 squadron. As I made my way past several unattended offices facing the airfield it seemed after all that I was in the wrong place. An airman emerged from hangar's main entrance. Surprised by my presence he asked me why I was not in bed like the rest of the crews.

'I have just been posted here. Where are the crew rooms?'

'They are all here,' he waved his hand across the doorways. 'But you won't find anyone today after last night's maximum effort.'

'Why, what happened?'

'Where have you been, Sarge? We've spent whole week preparing for this first 1000 aircraft raid and everything was airborne last night except the kitchen sink. I believe we have flattened Munich properly this time. Come back tomorrow, things might be back to normal.'

I found Sergeants Mess equally abandoned. A large anteroom full of empty chairs, a few newspapers and magazines left open here and there on the tables, and closed shutters of the bar gave an almost ghostly impression. It was nearly lunchtime and I decided to stay. Soon, bored with the scene I wandered in vain from table to table impatiently waiting for a meeting with just one member of the squadron to fill my inquiring mind of who is who and where do I fit in. On my first day in Lindholme I found nothing except, tucked away near the bar, a well used gramophone with only one, also well worn record of the thirties saucy tune ' . . . but she had to go and loose it at the Astor,' the refrain which stayed with me as an imprint of war time nostalgia to date.

Early next morning I was outside the same offices in time to see an orderly unlock the doors. A few minutes later the whole place was buzzing with activity as ground staff and aircrew of all ranks began to fill the premises, the latter easily recognisable more by their conversation rather than their uniform insignia. I followed the clerks through the steel door marked Squadron Administration and, having introduced myself, I was duly given half a dozen forms to fill in with the personal details which were relentlessly required on every new station. The choice of next posting was always a bit of a laugh but the address of next of kin was to us Poles more of a dilemma. Next, the long awaited meeting in the crew room a few doors away. As I walked into the noisy smoke filled room, conversation temporarily stopped while everyone's eyes scrutinised the newcomer with an instinctive herd-like assessment which I would have found embarassing had it lasted more than a second more. 'Hi, are you Jacek Blocki?' Voice came with an outstretched hand from one of the pilots nearest to me.

'Hi, that's me.'

'Here, meet the gang.'

After a lot of handshaking and some light hearted questions and comments about my choice of a career, I suddenly felt at home and joined in the general melée of verbal exchanges. One hour later I was standing to attention in front of my Squadron commander who introduced me to the more serious side of the squadron's life. The Polish Air Force Major, wearing Squadron Leader's rank, cut a figure of a relaxed uncle rather than a warrior but there was no doubt about his authority. His name was Sniegula.

'Stand at ease, welcome to 305. There is nothing romantic about

A senior pilot at the age of 20 on the front row of a somewhat decimated aircrew.

this job and you will follow orders implicitly. As soon as your skiving crew arrive you will go through a quick conversion course to Wellington Mk.II, which we are equipped with, then you will start operations with a screen pilot who, with a bit of luck, will show you how it is done. Report to 'B' Flight, they will look after you. Have you been fed and accommodated?'

'Yes sir.'

'Good, that's all then, Blocki.'

I saluted, turned around and left his office knowing I had a boss.

Before my crew's arrival next day I spent the time visiting dispersal points around the airfield meeting some of the groundcrew and admiring the largest twin engine bombers of the Royal Air Force which were powered by Mk.X Rolls Royce engines, The following week our conversion started with circuits and bumps, two daylight cross-countries and ended with only one hour of local night flying. During that time two of our squadron crews failed to return from a raid on Essen and for the first time I witnessed the serious side of life around me, reflected in the removal of the personal belongings of the missing crews from their individual lockers and a sudden lack of the everyday humourous sarcasm in the crew rooms. Even though I hardly knew the chaps I found this atmosphere infectious and began to cling closer to my own crew whose apprehension made them equally vulnerable despite our whole-hearted companionship. Fortunately, the chief of Bomber Command known as Bomber Harris did not believe in giving aircrew too much time in thinking about their future and only one day after our conversion I sat in the operations room next to my screen pilot Flying Officer Jan Borowski with the rest of my lads. Wide eyed we took in every word of the briefing officer who obviously has performed this task several times before and who added some humour to the proceedings.

'Easy job tonight, chaps . . .' but before he could take second breath a chorus of veterans behind me sounded disbelief, 'Not another one?!' Unpurturbed he continued: '. . . target for tonight is Emden,' he removed the cover from a large hanging map behind him and pointed at the German coast. 'The aim is to hit docks there and any shipping within. You are all carrying 500 pounders and after the briefing I want you to take a good look at the photographs of the target area displayed here. As you will hear from the Met man skies should be clear and identification should not be difficult but remember, there will be 80 other aircraft aiming at the same spot within half an hour of each other so constant look out is essential.' He pressed on with details of the likely German defences and route itself which Jan and I copied carefully and after answering few questions from the assembled crews he concluded: 'You have plenty of time, this being the shortest night of the year, take off at 2230. Enjoy your supper.'

In company of three other squadron crews we had our first operational meal of egg and bacon, a real treat in the days of strict food rationing. It was more than satisfying and no one seemed at all anxious while the light hearted back-chat lasted. Later in the hangar the atmosphere changed visibly. In front of one's own locker, dressing for the occasion and carefully placing personal belongings and identity items inside it, I was given time to think while separated from the crowd and discovered my first touch of instinctive fear which clouded all other thoughts. Throughout my operational flying that same feeling recurred at the same time of preparations and I learned to hate my locker.

Still in broad daylight a three tonner arrived outside the offices and we clambered on board in our leather, fur lined flying gear, helmets hanging round our necks and parachutes under our arms. The morale was restored.

The lorry made its way along the taxi way to the dispersal points where all the aircraft were parked and where all servicing, refueling and bombing up took place. After dropping off two other crews we arrived on a concrete pan, home of S for Sugar, its sooty black fuselage bearing the RAF roundel and the Polish red and white checkered square. She was almost new and her huge Merlins looked ready for action. She was a single seater which meant that her controls were available to one pilot only. It was decided therefore in advance that I would go not only as a second pilot but also as a bomb aimer and Stefan got his night off. In complete radio silence at 2215 Jan positioned the aircraft close to the taxi way and we waited impatiently for the green light from the caravan next to the runway. As the last sun rays disappeared over the horizon all four Wellingtons were lined up behind each other ready for take off. Runway lights supplemented by yellow flickering paraffin goosenecks were clearly visible when our turn came. The gradual roar of the engines reached their crescendo and the much heavier than air machine began its slow but dignified run towards the red lights ahead. With 2000 pounds of bombs and full fuel load she reluctantly lifted her tail first and did not take to the air until 200 yards from the end of the runway. Seeing my discomfort Jan casually picked up his oxygen mask-cum-microphone and reassured me: 'This is quite normal, wait till you get 4000 pounder strapped to your arse, that can be tricky.' My hand released its tension on the spar next to me and I peered into the darkness as instructed. Of course, all navigation lights had to be extinguished but there was always a chance of seeing the glow of the exhausts nearby and anyway we were all going in the same direction at similar speeds. Close to the target that's another matter . . . Slowly minutes passed as we climbed to the operational height of 18000 feet which is as high as our supercharged Merlins could take us. Through the powerful drum of the two engines, short but precise messages between the crew had a reassuring effect and the gunners especially did not feel neglected. Ten minutes before the target I moved down through the narrow passage to the bomb aimer's position and laid behind the bombsight on the thick perspex beneath. As soon as I adjusted the instrument's function Piotr in the front turret excitedly announced lights ahead.

'Standard greeting from the Gerry coastal ack-ack,' commented Jan.

Although I could not see anything from my position I could sense the tension rising as various messages of activity around us buzzed through the intercom.

'Five minutes to the target,' barks Prot.

'How are you doing down there Jacek?' asks the skipper.

'I am OK.' I reply, 'I am just beginning to see some lights below, could be fires, yes, I can see the town and the harbour now, almost dead ahead . . . left, left, steady, steady. Bomb doors open . . . Boy, they're getting angry down there, can you see all the tracers getting near . . . steady.'

While I continued with my patter my stomach muscles contracted involuntarily each time a multicoloured ack-ack shell accelerated towards my exposed belly.

'Right a bit . . . steady . . . bombs gone!'

I felt the aircraft instantly bank to port and I struggled back upstairs, parachute weighing a ton. I sat again next to Jan panting with excitement: 'Wasn't that terrific? They'll never catch us now.'

We began to descend. Ahead, complete darkness, above, millions of stars. 'Funny,' I said, 'we never noticed them on the way out.'

Jan ignored my utterings completely. 'Here,' he pointed to his seat, 'take over, Jacek, the ops bloke was right, it was an easy one.'

'S' for Sugar

CHAPTER 5

Home From Home

Before the end of July I had finished my operational apprenticeship and became the first pilot of my own crew and my own Wellington, still S for Sugar, airframe No 8343. Throughout, she was meticulously maintained by the same ground crew led by a Sergeant fitter, two Corporal fitters, one airframe, the other engines, who adopted the aircraft as their own property. Equally proud to belong were three more airmen of various qualifications who completed the team. In retrospect, I am certain that my survival during those trying days was mainly due to my ground crew's dedication and skill. On take off, for example, one murmur in an engine with 24 sparking plugs firing, valves and pistons disposing of gallons of 100 octane petrol every few seconds while the aircraft is defying the laws of gravity with a maximum load of fuel and a 4000 pound bomb sticking out of the belly with the bomb-doors removed, could have only resulted in another deep crater close to the airfield. To my great shame and because a pilot's log book does not cater for the names of the ground crew their identity will rest unannounced. Of course, in competition with other ground crews our team argued that their aircrew was the best on the island which, needless to say, was short in substance, although in those days, even I believed that I was the best trained pilot flying the best aeroplane.

In the meantime my personal life was very much affected by the arrival of two letters which came within a week of each other. The first one, forwarded by our headquarters in London, was a brief note from Rafal giving his address in Scotland and asking for my whereabouts in the UK. So he did make it with the Polish Army after all! I was delighted. The second letter was in a shape of small brown envelope re-addressed three times via London, Bramcote and Lindholme. Inside I found a complimentary slip from Thomas Cook & Son Ltd., Berkeley Street, London, W1. and a card printed in German titled: Kriegsgefangenenpost, Postkarte. I recognise the writing instantly. It's my father's! Good old dad, he made it as well . . . I did not know whether to cry or laugh. I had a closer look at the print. Below my name there are details of the sender: Oberst. Stefan Blocki, Gefangenennummer 41.BIV/kl.2., Oflag VI E, Dorsten in Westfalen, Deutschland. Initially addressed to Lissabon, Postfach 506, Portugalien, the card contained few hand written words expressing hope that both sons are well and eagerly awaiting news. Well, the text did not matter at all but the end of months of un-certainty left me in a state of elation. After answering the card through Lisbon my mind returned to Warsaw recollecting years of adolescence, frequently with a feeling of remorse, for the first signs of maturity and my often rebellious attempts at teenage independence must have been, to say the least, trying for parents and tutors alike. Looking for excuses I could not help remembering that some of those misunderstandings were not helped by the existing generation gap between father and son.

Poor sophisticated Papa! The fifth son born to a rather prosperous family in the days of great Austro-Hungarian empire, which in its collection of mid-European states included a large chunk of divided Poland, my father was dispatched at a young age to the Vienna Military Academy. Generally, Poles like the Hungarians, were treated as second class citizens but exceptions were made in cases of special attributes such as intelligence, aristocratic origin or wealth. The best example of these exceptions was a Polish Count with one of the richest holdings in southern Poland and owner of several Lippizaner horses, symbols of great importance to the upper crust in Vienna, who became a successful Minister of Minorities, personally appointed by the Emperor himself. There were no such advantages in my father's background. Nevertheless, at the end of his training he was commissioned in one of the select Austrian regiments. Three years before World War I came promotion to the rank of Captain and he was soon thrust into the courtly Viennese life of gaiety and music.

In his own words, nothing as nice as this lasts forever and with tensions mounting throughout Europe, especially in the Balkans, his regiment arrived at the beginning of 1914 in a notorious trouble spot called Sarayevo. There was little chance, father told me once, of preventing the assassination of Grand Duke Ferdinand which precipitated the Great War because for every two citizens of that country one could find three bandits ready to kill anybody for any reason.

The end of the war in 1918 resulted in the disintegration of the Austrian Empire and the rebirth of an independent Poland. Thirty-two year old dashing Major Stefan Blocki [remember to pronounce C as TS] returned to his native land and married 18 year old Wanda, in the fashion in those days, the daughter of a Polish lawyer and a Viennese lady of society. In between gay soirees laced with waltzes, operettas, Mozart, and Chopin, two sons were conceived, myself making an appearance on Christmas Eve 1921.

Perhaps things would have run smoother 14 years later if I have not befriended Tadeusz Bergman, the only Jew in a classroom of 30 boys, whose father owned a Fiat car agency in Warsaw and whose upbringing was entirely different to mine. While he knew everything about Hollywood and American jazz, I was still living a century ago. When Auntie Zofia, another rare, modern individual in the back-woods of Poland, persuaded my father to buy a new gramophone, I proudly played a borrowed record of Fats Waller, whose piano playing and sense of humour appealed to me instantly. Alas, after only two renditions of Alligator Crawl this kind of music was never again allowed to disturb one's intellect in our house. My disappointment was complete and I retired hurt into the more sympathetic world of my Jewish friend. Only a few months later my unconforming sixteen year old mind declared war on the Church of Rome. This unwise move in a country consisting of 99 per cent Roman Catholics had me nearly expelled from the college, and caused my father to apologise to the Board of Directors and the clergy. This he obviously did not like doing.

'I don't give a damn which God you believe in,' he hollered, 'you're not dragging me through this again and I am not wasting another cent on your education unless you write a sincere letter of apology to Father Dominik. Do you hear me?!'

I knew instantly that he meant business but, even so, I foolishly tried to defend my stance: 'But Father I have only written what's true . . .'

'You heard what I said, get out!'

This I did. I picked up my overcoat and ran away from home into the snow covered streets of Warsaw. After all, I had been asked to write an essay on any religious subject of my choice as a pre-emptive exercise to matriculation. The fact that I doubted the sincerity of some popes and cardinals, whose advertised vocation and love of humanity did not match their lust for power and wealth, was not likely to start a revolution. Certainly the Christian values often imposed by torture during the Inquisition or the roasting alive of dissidents in the name of God were not in the curriculum of a respected Warsaw college and my essay was not what the strict Polish school inspectors wanted to read in 1938. Stubbornly convinced that I had corrected a major historical inexactitude I was not going to apologise to anyone.

Twelve hours later, at 5 o'clock in the morning, frozen to the marrow after a sleepless night on a park bench by the ice covered banks of the Vistula river, my determination weakened considerably and I sought refuge in the warm arms of my dear Auntie Zofia. At that stage I learned what a lot of panic was created by my departure and with my subdued pater, who was now the main recipient of the women's wrath, I was welcomed back to a much more understanding family atmosphere. Mother and Aunt Zofia confronted also an embarrassed headmaster in my presence who shyly retreated from his original stand and quickly accepted my verbal apology for causing so much fuss. The great pity of it all was that from then on, father and I failed to communicate on any subject of wordly importance although on occasions he did allow me to partner him at bridge.

Once again all the thoughts of home were pushed into the background when the mighty executives of Bomber Command decided to move 305. Squadron to Hemswell on the Lincolnshire Ridge. A move which was completed before the end of August. By this time the bombing of Germany became more intense and the crew of S for Sugar started to take a lot of physical and mental punishment. Two or even three consecutive nights amidst the searchlights and the extremely effective 88 millimeter guns of the German defences made our survival a No.1 priority. In my case, Lady Luck blessed me throughout with her attentions and, as squadron losses mounted with sickening regularity, I soon became a screen pilot. I then shared experience as a 20 year old between the replacement crews, God bless them, and the remains of my fading regulars. First to leave me were Prot, the navigator and Stefan the bomb aimer. It was my 11th operation, target Saarbrucken, nothing as nasty as the Ruhr we thought. 'Only light ack ack expected,' said the briefing chap. At 16000 feet and in close company with some 200 other bombers, we arrived in the target area still intact when all the hell lets loose. There was no doubt they were 88s. Consecutive quick flashes on the ground, soon followed by massive explosions all around us produced an outburst of voices from both turrets: 'Look out, ack ack to the left! . . . ack ack in front! Did you see that! The bastards got him . . .' In the intense white light of the searchlights there were, clearly visible, the falling remains of one of our aircraft trailing flames and smoke. Next, an instant powerful explosion rips through the fabric fuselage of our Wellington lifting it abruptly at a peculiar angle. No reply from Stefan. I jettison the bombs and try to stabilise the aircraft. Quick messages on the intercom prove that at least we are all alive, although voices sound shaken. Stefan's intercom is cut off somewhere along the line. With both wings flapping the holed, draughty plane bounces through the turbulence created by exploding shells while I turn sharply for home. There is another flash beneath us followed by a piercing noise from the port engine coming directly into my left ear. The rev counter spins twice round. For a few seconds everything shakes around me then one more violent shudder and the propeller next to my face disappears into the night. I wait for an explosion . . . nothing happens.

'Steady lads,' my voice sounds like an echo from someone else's throat and I feel sweat trying to escape from underneath my flying helmet, 'parachutes ON. DON'T jump yet, she is still flying and there is no fire. I am going to drop a few thousand feet to accelerate a bit out of this hell-hole. Prot, give me the course to the nearest coast, we'll see how things go.'

Two minutes later there is no more war and only the sound of the starboard engine drumming steadily in the distance. All controls are responding and she is happy doing 150 mph in a steady descent. Soon we are over Belgium and then Holland. Now passing 8000 feet, the moment of decision. What will happen if I level out? Will she maintain height? Up to now no one to my knowledge has seriously practiced single engine flying over great distances. The theory of flight including asymmetric flying was not high on the agenda in the rushed wartime training. Various ideas, such as 'never turn towards the dead engine' were not very convincing even to those who taught me how to fly.

I level out and increase power on the starboard engine to find out that at an indicated 95 to 100 mph, which is all our wounded Sugar is capable of now, I can maintain height but only just. Below that speed she starts being woolly, with rudder control fully extended. As we pass the coastline I share my findings with the anxious crew.

'We are about to cross the Dutch coastline and that leaves us with at least 120 miles to do over the North Sea. As you can feel she is just about holding her own and I think it is possible to get her home but no guarantees . . . the alternative is obvious: while we are still over 7000 feet high I can turn around and we can all bale out over Holland in an orderly fashion. How about that?'

Almost in unison voices ring out in my ears. 'Carry on Jacek, you can make it!'

Half an hour later, while Henryk prostrate below is helping my right foot to apply a strong steady pressure on the rudder, I get another surprise. Piotr, who has just left front turret to defrost his body after spending hours in the coldest part of the Wellington makes his way to the navigator's table and reports that the back of Stefan's flying jacket is covered in blood and he wants to know if it is all right to unstrap his parachute. Himself and Prot get to work on the reluctant victim and find a two inch cut behind the ear piece of the flying helmet filled with congealed blood. Since the patient is very much conscious and makes remarks like, ' . . .so that's why my intercom isn't working,' we decide to leave things as they are.

It is now 6 o'clock and the first signs of daylight appear above the horizon on my right. I decide to ease the constantly demanding

Look at the size of that engine! My 'S' for Sugar, Summer 1942

attention to the instruments required for level flight and commence a shallow descent. She is much happier now gaining 10 mph while loosing 100 feet per minute. The coast of Lincolnshire comes into view in broad daylight, the Humber estuary a perfect pinpoint. Shouts of 'HURRAH' and radio silence is broken. I talk to Hemswell and request straight in approach for emergency landing. An excited voice assures me everything is ready. I leave the flaps and undercarriage until the runway is in sight, not being sure whether either would operate. Now at 1000 feet and two miles to go I lower both, the crew bracing themselves in crash positions. Nose down and floating like a fat goose Sugar touches down way up the runway while I try to slow things down with full use of the brakes. We skid into the grassy overshoot area followed by fire vehicles and ambulances and come face to face with the airfield boundary hedge, still in one piece. As I unstrap myself Henryk with a loud sigh of relief is the first to grab me. Our ground crew make their way through the crowd of would be rescuers, and beat the Flight Commander, Duty Pilot and other officials to the ladder below. 'Well done Jacek, we knew you would make it!' Suddenly, all the stress is gone and I feel great.

Stefan was whisked off to the Station Sick Quarters where medics discovered that his skull was shrapnel-proof although he had to stay there because of blood loss. The rest of us finished in the Ops Room for the de-briefing laced with extra rations of rum and coffee before crashing out into the dreamland for a day.

Despite being treated by all with sudden unexpected respect, I soon realised how much we owed that night to sheer luck and I tried in vain to reduce my fame stricken crew's cockiness. Shrapnel which penetrated the reduction gears in front of the port engine disintegrated main casing, hence the loss of the propeller. The violent surge in revs could have easily caused an internal fire, but it did not. Had the prop stayed on jammed with the ceased gears enormous drag on the port side would have prevented any chance of maintaining lateral control of the aircraft and at the very best we would have now been giving the Germans our names, ranks and service numbers. I was also thankful that the Merlin's streamlined construction had reduced the asymmetric drag even further. Nevertheless, when trying to explain all this to the lads covered in glycol and grease inside the hangar where S for Sugar was under-going serious repairs, including an engine change, I failed to convince them that my part in this lucky escape was nothing to write home about.

Two days later she was ready for an air test, 33 holes repaired, fuselage resprayed and a brand new Rolls Royce engine in the port nacelle. Human problems, on the other hand, could not be rectified so easily. Stefan was transferred to hospital for further checks and during the same week Prot's prolonged battle with the doctors to conceal his stomach ulcer came out in the open when it suddenly burst after few beers in the Officers' Mess. This event which initially created some sick humour within the squadron with references to eggs before flying, in fact ended his flying career. Perhaps he was lucky, who knows?

As the intensity of bombing increased so did our losses. After the fifth aircraft had disappeared over Germany since my arrival on the squadron, new crews came forth and it was my turn again to look confident while showing them how it is done. Whether I fooled them or not I am not certain but my ever increasing fear after one more lucky escape drove me to superstition; behaviour quite common among the survivors yet never advertised in the open. Another close confrontation with the 88s, this time over Essen, resulted in several more holes in the Wellington's almost indestructible geodetic construction and on return in the early hours of the morning I found my steel hangar locker slightly ajar. At first, some nasty thoughts run through my mind until I found all my worldly possessions intact and it was obvious that I had failed to turn the key. I retired to bed only to be wakened up at 4p.m. by loud knocking on the door and the unkind voice of the Duty Sergeant announcing briefing in two hours time and take off at eight. It is hard to describe what ugly feelings that sort of treatment produces in a disorientated mind which only a few hours before had congratulated itself on being alive and hoped for a prolonged siesta. Still, not without a good deal of moaning and swearing, I managed to collect my reluctant heroes, and after breakfast cum flying supper, we were ready once again for the bad news. Back in the hangar I faced my hated steel locker for the second time that day, and after depositing all my identifiable belongings, one thought stopped me in my tracks. 'Remember last night? That's an omen . . . if you lock it you may not come back!' I did not lock it that evening or ever again through my remaining operations. The omen was reinforced after the safety equipment airman handed me a jagged piece of shrapnel at the briefing: 'Here Sarge, we found it this morning imbedded in your parachute, it was only two inches from your arse. You can keep it.' I kept it with a good deal of pride, although the locker affair remained a secret even to Henryk and remainder of my original crew.

Another month went by and the beginning of October brought with it the typical autumn mixture of gales, rains, low cloud and icing. Most of our weather information over Germany came mainly from the returning crews and was quite reliable if not complete, but harnessing of elements into 100 per cent accurate forecasting was no more possible in 1942 than it is now. Most of our aircraft were quite unable to climb above the weather. Ploughing through frontal systems in complete darkness, except for lightning or electrical discharges often accompanied by heavy turbulence and the icing up of wings and propellers caused additional Bomber Command losses and restricted the number of operations. Our propaganda machine, designed for the purpose of confusing the enemy and the maintenance of the nation's morale, made sure that any serious set back such as Dunkirk or Narvik would appear as bad news to the other side, so heavy losses in Bomber Command had to be adjusted accordingly. Only occasionally did sad facts emerge in their entirety and, in the case of one costly raid on Stuttgart were revealed to me personally.

Detailed at a short notice to bring back one of our stranded crews after a prang in Manston I took off soon after sunrise heading for the Garden of England. Flying at low level we crossed the Thames estuary into Kent, and while admiring the views, Henryk was first to notice a long trail of freshly scarred fields terminating in the wreckage of a four engine Stirling. Nearer to Manston, the countryside was littered with crashed aeroplanes resembling more a huge mushroom farm than the approaches to an airfield. Air Traffic Control warned me of the obstructions which in any case were clearly visible from the air and I landed between a tailless Stirling and a wheels-up Wellington. The two must have collided on the ground at night and presented a grim picture of the chaotic events which must have taken place only a few hours ago. On the way back all was revealed by the surviving crew.

Some 400 bombers took part in a major raid and headed South East into winds forecast at 50 to 60mph reducing groundspeeds of most types to about 100 mph. As expected it took four and a half hours flying to the target and everyone looked forward to a rapid return home. That hope was soon shattered by a freak change in the weather pattern over France when a small but vicious secondary depression moved quickly through Holland into the North Sea changing the upper wind to strong north-westerly. Three hours later still over Belgium our chaps began to run out of fuel, and then panic! The fact that our crew were in the leading group saved them because the contrary winds did not catch them until half way back home. Still, the nail biting remainder of the flight ended with fuel gauges reading zero and a spluttering starboard engine on finals.

'You should have heard the R/T,' said one of them.

'I can imagine,' Henryk, being a wireless operator himself, chipped in, 'was it you who cut the Sterling's tail off?'

'Sure, fancy leaving the bastard in the middle of the airfield without lights. Lucky for them, they must have run like hell seeing what was going on.'

At lunch time the BBC announced the successful destruction of industrial targets in Stuttgart adding that unfortunately 58 of our aircraft failed to return. Human casualties were craftily never mentioned in these bulletins. Nevertheless, we knew the losses of that night could be doubled, for it was likely that a similar number of aircraft to those we saw in the Kentish fields were also incapable of taking any further part in the war effort. A few more morale shattering cock-ups like the disappearance in one night of a complete Australian squadron based in Binbrook, 10 miles north of Hemswell and equipped with the same Wellingtons Mk. II as ours, must have had some effect on our leaders. It was then no surprise that Lincolshire Ridge became a much quieter place, for at least a fortnight, that is. Leave passes were signed and the White Hart in the centre of Lincoln, full to capacity with thirsty airmen, ran out of beer every night.

I spent three days in Scotland where I found my brother performing secretarial duties with a Polish regiment in a place called Auchtermuchty. Our first reunion since Poland ended in my introduction to the Highland Dew after which, despite the welcome and loveliness of this unspoiled country, I was more than ready for the return to England. Back in my room in Hemswell I found a scribbled note from Henryk inviting me to follow him to Blackpool. It finished by saying: 'Don't worry about accommodation. My old landlady will be glad to have you.' It took all next day to get to the west coast, courtesy of the wartime railways with changes in Sheffield and Manchester, but it was worth it.

My first visit to the Nadins was an instant success. Partially due to the patriotism of Jim, a 14–18 war veteran who enjoyed being seen in company of a decorated pilot and maybe because of the way I asked Alice if she would allow me to take her youngest daughter to the pictures, I found myself attended to in a most relaxing family atmosphere. The mainspring of my attachment to these lovely people lay, however, in the spontaneous mutual attraction between Hilda and myself. Certainly not discouraged by her parents, she accompanied me for the rest of the week to Blackpool's luxurious cinemas, the Winter Gardens ballroom and even to a spectacular show in the Opera House, something so new to me I felt I was floating on the clouds of a wonderland. We laughed and giggled as she pretended to run away ahead of me on the windswept promenade, only to be caught in my arms again and again. Soon we were holding hands, staring at each other and sneaking an occasional kiss but only after my lovely partner in crime made sure no one would notice. Her beautiful golden tresses prompted me to call her Honey and Honey she stayed. In the meantime, poor Henryk was relegated to the second division although, on the quiet, he did enjoy being spoilt by Mum and Dad who took him out to the local hostelry. On the last night before our departure all of us went out together and after few more drinks back home, Henryk began to offload his most depressing inner feelings which only alcohol can expose. Sitting next to me he put his arm around my neck and turned unsteadily to the rest of company: 'You are looking at the bessht pilot in the Polish Air Forsshe,' he blurred out, ' . . . pity I cannot finish my tour with him . . . because without Jacek I am a dead duck. I'll not come back, you'll sshee . . .'

'Don't be so bloody silly!' I interrupted trying to lift him off the settee. 'It's high time you went to bed. Sorry about this folks, I'll see he is all right.'

It was a sad ending to a perfect visit but like the rest of the family not for a moment did I take Henryk's woes seriously. With promises of millions of letters and to return at the first opportunity, I left my newly found home and managed to deliver Henryk as far as the boarding house steps where his motherly landlady took over.

Unfortunately Hemswell was still in the same place and waiting for us. For the first time in my life I began to realise how precious even one week's happiness can be on this earth when someone tries to kill you so often and with such persistency. It never occurred to me to do anything else but continue flying. The motivation never wavered although I had to ask myself a few pertinent questions, especially after a raid on Hamburg, which took place only two days after my return from Blackpool. It was the last time I flew with the remnants of my original crew. The Germans greeted us with the usual concentrated fire from Heligoland to the target which we made after weaving above layer clouds brilliantly illuminated by the full moon and delivered our 4000 pounder exactly on top of the pathfinder's flares. Funny thing about the Krauts, they never stopped firing, not even after the massive explosion of our block buster down below and I did not waste any time before turning away towards the comparative safety of the North Sea. Both gunners began to congratulate each other on a trouble free run when, without any warning from Kazik in the rear turret, two white hot tracers shot past on both sides of the fuselage, level with my head, and dipped ahead out of sight. One shout of 'Christ!' on the intercom indicated that someone's been hit and instinctively I pushed the control column fiercely forward and right. The next second, dark shadow of an aeroplane swooped above me nearly as fast as the tracers and disappeared to port in a steep turn. In almost a vertical dive I entered the cloud 5000 feet below us and breathed loudly a sigh of relief

'I think we lost him . . . Hell! That was a close one. Henryk, check the rear turret, let's hope Kazik is still with us.'

Henryk came back after a minute or so and plugged himself into the intercom. 'He's still there, but he doesn't move and there is a hole in the turret above his head. I need some help to get him out of there, strange . . . he doesn't seem to be injured.' As soon as Kazik was brought out of the turret and made comfortable by the navigator's table it became apparent that he was suffering from severe shock. His speech was an uncoordinated stammer while his wide open eyes stared fixed into space. Whether he heard our subsequent review of events we could not tell even though we tried to make it as light hearted as possible. It was no secret that for quite some time now the Luftwaffe were expecting to receive the JU 88 twin engine night fighter with two 20 millimetre cannons mounted in its wings but it seemed unfair to us that they finally decided to try out this nasty piece of work on our S for Sugar. I reckoned that the Gerry pilot tried too hard for a kill in almost daylight visibility and opened up much to close to his target, leaving us snug between two tracers. Only one shell grazed our rear turret leaving a crack two inches above Kazik's head.

83

'Aren't you bloody lucky,' said Henryk without getting any response. In reality our return to base turned out to be a most uncomfortable experience even though the stricken gunner recovered most of his composure by the time we landed 3 hours later.

He was taken to Sick Quarters and came back after 48 hours under observation, making it clear to me in a very subdued manner that he did not give a damn what the doctors say but he is not going inside a Wellington ever again. Two weeks later Kazik was posted, victim of the infamous LMF (Lack of Moral Fibre). That was the only treatment for mental stress available to the bloody minded system which was until then guided by the prevailing ignorance of the subject within the medical profession. Still, I suppose, posting and reduction in rank was at least a humane improvement compared with the First World War policy of shooting every tenth man. It was not until two years later that I heard of Kazik's whereabouts. After serving his country on 14 operational flights he finished the war as a cook in an airman's mess.

Worse was to come. Bomber Command bosses prompted by ever increasing casualties and resulting loss of morale on the flying stations decided to sacrifice a number of senior officers from both Group Headquarters. They were distributed evenly between different squadrons presumably to emphasize that those who plan and give orders do care. The Wing Commander who arrived in Hemswell from No. 1 Group Bawtry was given a few hours conversion flying and on 3rd November with a motley crew of 305 Squadron remnants took off for Germany and disappeared without trace. The heartbreaking thing for me was that Piotr and Henryk were part of that crew. I thought for weeks about Henryk's premonition way back in Blackpool and was sad for the Nadins who received another telegram starting with the words: 'I am sorry to inform you . . .' After all it was the third boy to whom they had opened their home and who they would never see again. Now, left without the remainder of my trusty pals, I felt more lonely than ever and the standard tour of 30 operations seemed impossible to achieve. Meanwhile all the Wellingtons Mk.II were replaced with Mk.IV's and I said good bye to S for Sugar, block busters and hairy take offs.

Things could only get better and predictably they did. Unknown to me, the last replacement crew from Bramcote had their pilot grounded on medical grounds and I was surprised to become an almost instant substitute. With lighter loads and the more economical Pratt and Whitney Wasp radial engines we were able to reach targets beyond the Ruhr and on one occasion, taking off from Tangmere on the south coast, we dropped four 200 pounders on Turin with hardly a shot fired.

My correspondence with Honey acquired a much lighter outlook but another card from my father brought with it somewhat sinister news in the change of address. As soon as I saw Oflag 2, Duisburg in the reply section, I realised that only two weeks ago I was dropping bombs on that place. Swines, I thought, fancy putting a prisoner of war camp next to our favourite target, I am in a cleft stick here! Fortunately, the role of our Polish bomber squadrons was changing rapidly now, thanks to the unsustainable losses and shortage of personnel replacements and I never went to the Rhur again. Father survived the bombings and on his 55th birthday was released from prison. He returned to Warsaw in time for Easter 1943, which must have been a godsend to Mamusia. At the same time I completed my last 6 operational flights tearing low level in total darkness across the Brest peninsula and dropping magnetic mines around the approaches to St Nazaire and Lorient, both principal bases of the German submarine Atlantic fleet. This was an excellent final navigational exercise because of the precision required in positioning the deep sea mines, as well as the avoidance of the heavily defended coastline and harbours themselves.

Now, at the ripe age of 21and looking even younger I begin, with a lot of patience, to cultivate a mustache hoping to attain some respect as a seasoned warrior. After 30 weeks of a blissful time with Honey, not forgetting several pints and snooker with Dad, I am considered to be good enough to instruct pilots on how to fly Wellingtons in an Operational Training Unit at Finningley in Yorkshire. Four months of intensive programme with three students followed, packing in as much as 6 hours of circuits and bumps in one night. Then, it is decided to send me on a Flying Instructors course to No.2 FIS Montrose. What a relief. Having clocked up 600 hours of night flying in my first 1000 I am seeing daylight at last, also a toy of a single engine, a fully aerobatic Harvard. I am also promoted to Flight Sergeant and with two ribbons on my chest I feel quite mature. Long before the end of this exciting course I am informed that my next destination will be an officers training school run by the Polish cavalry regiment in Scotland. I expressed my surprise in the crew room full of English instructors and students. 'Oh,' says one, 'they are probably grooming you for the Chief of Staff, when you get back to Poland,' and everyone burst out laughing. It was immediately obvious that aircrew sense of humour has a common touch of sarcasm regardless of nationality. Apart from more important things in Montrose, I learned also how to respond to it.

All the time I spent away from Honey, plus the caring family atmosphere and sense of belonging made me hurry back to Blackpool as soon as the course was over. This time I decided to take the bull by the horns. I bought a cluster of diamonds for Honey's finger and stupidly asked if she would marry me. She melted in my arms and several kisses later I realised that my nervousness and anxiety leading to this event was quite unnecessary and we were truly engaged. Each day after seemed to last for only an hour and we walked on air until the dreaded moment of my departure.

In contrast, the long journey back to Scotland seemed never ending and my arrival there, on a cold and drizzly evening, added to my feeling of emptiness and melancholy. I trudged down the crowded platform of Perth railway station, kit bag under my arm, towards a dimly lit sign saying WAY OUT, pressed on all sides by a long queue of uniformed humanity when I heard a familiar voice.

'Well, I'll be damned! It is Jacek, isn't it?'

It was Vitold. A barrage of questions followed during which I discovered that Vic, as he is known now, has finally finished his operational flying from Cammeringham, also in Lincolnshire, and is here to attend the same commissioning school as myself. Some hours later in the company of a few other candidates, mainly young aircrew, we arrived in the back of an Army lorry outside a stately home with a grand driveway and an even more impressive entrance. This place, converted for its war time use and stripped of all valuables, consisted of endless corridors and large staircases leading to several rooms on two floors where we were accommodated. Kitchens, manned by the

Army cooks and the dining hall were down in the cellars from which a permanent smell of porridge and kippers oozed gently upwards. It was there, next morning at breakfast, that Vic and I were stunned to find Jurek.

'I can't believe it, this is too much of a coincidence, who let you in?' I asked, provoking an equally smart answer.

'Steady, junior. You are addressing an officer and in future I expect to be called sir!'

We shook hands warmly and Vic gave him a hug. 'So where is your rank, you rascal.'

'You see, mates, I beat you to it, I am leaving this palace the day after tomorrow. We are passing out today, sorry I have to leave you now, I have to get ready and all that, but I will see you tonight when they let you free, probably after six.'

All of that day Vic and I learned how to shout 'SIR' loud and clear to our instructors while we collected army combat gear and marched up and down the parkland lanes in pouring rain with a lot of comment about an untidy and undisciplined Air Force from the tough Sergeant in the rear.

'I thought you'd be knackered,' said Jurek after finding us stretched out on our bunkbeds after the supper. 'You must have been spoiled wicked in Bomber Command, long hours, long sleep and no excitement . . .'

I was in no mood for joking and bit the bait: 'And what would you know about it, you slept every bloody night and most of the day except for hopping to 20000 feet and back in an hour to wave your scarf in front of the girls.'

Jurek pretended to yawn. 'OK, OK, you brave lot, and which one of you bombed Dublin last year then? That couldn't have been easy.'

The trump card which became the fighter boy's favourite witticism in the friendly inter-Command competition was a reference to an unpublicised effort by one of the unrecognised Lincolnshire based aircraft flying a course exactly 180 degrees out and then mistaking Dublin for Bremen!

I had to be sharp and responded with similar wit: 'Good God, how on earth did you discover our most treasured secret. At least we are not pretending to be perfect like your clan who don't even know there is a compass in the Spitfire!' Here Vic came to the rescue. 'By the way, Jurek, compass or no compass, have you found a nice filly yet on your travels down South?'

'Listen fellows, just now I am trying to avoid females like a plague. Most of them are willing for a reason. Not so long ago three of our chaps came back from a sortie in London with dreamy eyes and the same cock and bull story. Each found a girl that's different. I tell you boys, beware, when anyone tells you she is different, they're hooked! All three of them are engaged now.'

'How sad,' said Vic and I said nothing.

Jurek stretched his legs out on an empty bunk and glanced at me apologetically, 'Seriously though, I did notice your gongs when you arrived, was it worth it?'

'Hard to tell, some lads couldn't take it and who can blame them. One night- clean sheets and service next night: shrapnel. Pavlov says that even dogs can't take similar treatment for long and after 9 months I have certainly had enough.'

Vic nodded his head in agreement, 'I wonder if those in the POW camps, and there must be plenty of them, are reflecting on this because the rest who died cannot come back to express an opinion, not that it would be considered or even published . . .'

'One night stands are published,' I interrupted, 'such as the Mohne Dam or the first raid on Berlin. Both brave efforts with heavy losses yet of no tactical value, just spectacular morale boosters.'

'That's the price of war,' says Jurek. 'After disasters in Africa and the Far East, such as the sinking of those two battleships by the Japanese cloth and bamboo bombers, it surprises me there is any morale left. Any other country would have surrendered by now, like the French. You should have seen the excitement and victory signs when they unwrapped me from the silk on Brighton beach after a German E-Boat managed to put a shell through my Spit over the Channel.'

'Did you get kissed?'

'Only by the two old ladies who apparently couldn't wait a day longer to adopt a hero whatever uniform he was in. That was a narrow escape, I tell you!'

Whether he was pulling our leg we shall never know now. One

thing was certain. After this conversation, the news of my engagement had to wait a little bit longer.

The following evening Jurek came to see us again, this time to say good-bye. I could not contain myself any longer and took Honey's picture out of my pocket.

'Here take a look at this, what do you think?' Like an idiot I thought I needed second opinion.

Jurek always pretending to be a connoisseur of female shape allowed himself a dry comment: 'Not bad, not bad at all . . .'

Vic peeped over his shoulder. 'What do you mean, not bad? She is lovely! Where did you find her?'

'Sorry, lads, no more secrets can be revealed because I am going to marry her.' They both stared at me in disbelief while I tried to lessen the effect of my statement. 'Yes, I know, but she is different, really.'

Jurek took a deep breath. 'Well, who would have believed this, of all people! It looks, Vic, that we may have to come to the wedding as well, unless he changes his mind. I have to go now but don't forget to let me know how things develop.'

Ten weeks later Vic and I passed out after some torturous exercises in the Scottish hills. These included trench warfare with live ammunition, hand grenades and fixed heavy machine guns firing over our heads while we struggled through the mud towards imaginary enemies. Such treatment convinced us that we had chosen the right Service after all and we looked forward to any aircraft seat after miles in squeaky, iron hard Bren gun carriers. It was now the middle of November and I received an official communication stating that I have been commissioned in the rank of Pilot Officer with effect from 1st January. My initial gratification, however, was soon dispelled when I realised that anyway I would have been due for promotion to Warrant Officer a week before this on my 22nd birthday, a rank of respect and seniority rare at my age. On top of this I was heading for a financial disaster, expecting a pay increase of six pence a day but also the loss of practically free living in the Sergeants Mess plus free access to clothing stores. But, my family in Blackpool greeted the news with pride and elation, especially Alice who made sure that no one in the vicinity missed this bit of information. My future from now on was quite uncertain. Honey and I, therefore decided to get married as soon as possible, to the great delight of all the Nadins. I do not know how the females managed to organise such an event in the days of strict rationing when coupons were required even for shoe laces but they did.

On a clear but frosty morning on Monday, 13th December, I stood in my best blue Flight Sergeant's uniform at the arched alcove of St Paul's church waiting for my bride and reminding my best man Jurek and groomsman Vic about their responsibilities. Accompanied by my dear brother, they had all gone to bed after a blistering stag party only few hours before and the aroma of whisky and beer exhaled around me did nothing for my waning confidence. Nervously I watched a flower bedecked limousine pull up outside the entrance. Enhanced by the pale winter sun rays Honey appeared at the church gates guided by her father and attending bridesmaids. The breathtaking picture of lace and grace, golden hair adorned by silver sparkle and happiness beaming through the delicate veil prompted even Jurek to open his eyes wide. Rafal leaned over and whispered in my ear: 'My God, isn't she beautiful,' and I could only utter: 'I know, let's go in.'

The reception took place in a well known restaurant on the Promenade with some sixty guests enjoying proud Jim's generosity. One thing had to wait for a long time though and that was our honeymoon. After being granted special leave I was also told without any given reason that I was not to leave my place of address for even a day. During the following two weeks we stayed with Mum and Dad, lapping up every minute of togetherness that we were allowed to share and hoping that the world has forgotten us altogether.

Then, on Boxing Day, a telegram arrives: REPORT FOR DUTY RAF LYNEHAM STOP NOT LATER THAN 2 JANUARY STOP DOCUMENTATION FOLLOWS STOP.

The documentation which arrived next day consisted of a first class railway warrant in the name of PO J. Blocki and a reminder of my uniform and flying kit requirements. War time secrecy was in full swing and my initial destination was the only hint I was able to leave behind during the tearful departure from my loving haven. On arrival in Lyneham I finally discovered the sinister reason for all the grooming I had received during the past six months. No, it had nothing to do with the high office, although in the end I did meet the Polish Chief of Staff.

CHAPTER 6

Idealist At Work

I arrived in RAF Lyneham at midday after a twenty four hour train journey via London. The size of the station and the airfield with an amassment of terminal buildings, hangars and movement areas buzzing with activity could only be compared to a principal international airport with one exception: there was not a civilian aircraft in sight. Two hours later after commuting on foot between various offices from the guardroom to the Station Headquarters and back I could not find a single person interested in my arrival and retreated to a smart building bearing a sign in gold letters OFFICERS MESS. I deposited my meagre luggage in the reception and made more fruitless inquiries, terminating in the least helpful advice given by two seasoned aircrew residents who nonchalantly suggested that in this madhouse first priority is to find something to eat and somewhere to sleep. 'Stay here,' says one, 'have a beer when the bar opens and relax. When they need you they'll find you.' Easier said than done, I thought, but in the end my hunger overcame my glaring underconfidence as a brand new Pilot Officer surrounded by senior ranks. I sat down to dinner which consisted of a most uninviting meatless rissole, equally tasteless boiled potatoes and a slice of bread. The dissatisfied company at my table assisted their digestion by concentrating their conversation on the idiots in the recruiting branch who converted mechanics to cooks and vice versa. That evening in the bar after one morale lifting beer I explained my predicament to a Squadron Leader whose appearance and jovial manner was less off-putting than that of his companions. After a good deal of laughter at his remark that I should have been a navigator with such inadequate sense of direction, he told me that for blokes like me there was a place called Transit Reception. 'If you haven't found it in daylight, son, you won't find it now, it is miles from here on the other side of the airfield and you won't get any transport until morning. See if they can find you a bed here for tonight but be there at the crack of sparrows. They will tell you who awaits your pleasure and the best of luck to them.' In between some chuckling that followed I managed to utter: 'Thank you, sir,' before withdrawing smartly from any further embarrassment. It was then that I realised for the first time to what level of mediocrity my commission had dropped me into after achieving the respected rank of a Flight Sergeant Pilot.

To my relief the transit people did know about me. 'You should have been here yesterday, go straight away to the Flying Wing Ops, your crew is already there.' A little short of breath after swift walk through a maze of passages between the hangars I opened the door to a briefing room. Inside, the huge display of world wide maps and aerial photographs filled the windowless walls and a large podium at one end faced rows of writing desks, some occupied by busily plotting navigators. In the far corner a group of airmen stood closely together engaged in a discreet conversation. Even from that distance I immediately recognised the mannerisms of my compatriots and made my way towards them. 'You must be Jacek Blocki,' says the Flight Lieutenant bearing pilot wings. I nodded my head, 'That's me.'

'And where the hell have you been hiding? We expected you yesterday.' I tried to open my mouth but he beat me to it. 'Never mind that now.' He extended his hand. 'I am Stan Szostak, your Captain for this trip, meet Kazik Wunshe, our navigator and the rest of our crew, Witek, he plays with the radio, Wileniec, Jarecki and Malczyk our gunners and dispatchers.'

I shook hands with all of them in turn, and after the introductions, we moved to an adjacent room and sat around a chart table. Except for Wunshe all were Flight Sergeants, veterans of Bomber Command like myself. Stan and Kazik, both of the same rank, had gained their flying experience starting in the heady days of the early thirties in Poland and lately with Transport Command here in England.

'I bet you're dying to know what's all this is about,' started Stan. 'I arrived yesterday straight from a briefing in our Headquarters in London. We have been chosen to be part of the newly formed 1586. Special Duty Flight based in Italy. As you must know the Allies have progressed now past Naples and the whole boot of Italy is in our hands. This enables us to get nearer to the occupied countries including our own and in Churchill's own words "strike at the underbelly of Europe". The underground movements, particularly the Polish Home Army which is growing daily in numbers, need all the help they can get. The new Flight has been tasked to supply them with arms, ammunition, money and equipment essential to their survival, also . . .' he paused here for a moment, 'what will make our work particularly interesting, is that we will drop behind enemy lines specially trained experts, instructors and organisers. I am told that our aircraft is waiting here in Lyneham, it is a Liberator Mk.VI, known to Americans as a B-24. We have two weeks to get to know this ship and I've been given two copies of the Pilot's Notes and Manufacturer's Recommendations which I have already glanced through. Here, Jacek,' Stan produced a book the size of a bible, 'read it to the last detail. It is all the latest technology and you will soon discover why this aircraft requires two pilots. Finally, because of the clandestine nature of these operations I must impress upon you the need for secrecy about our work. I do not think the Germans will worry too much about the Geneva Convention if anyone involved in subversion is captured through wagging tongues or self glorifying letters to the girl friends.' He looked at his watch. 'Our bus to the dispersal should be here any minute now, we better continue our chat later.'

The 3-ton lorry took nearly half an hour to go round the perimeter track, dodging taxiing aircraft before turning off into a tarmacked dispersal a few hundred yards outside the airfield boundary. It halted noisily outside a Nissen hut and we eagerly jumped down to earth before anyone could lower the hinged steps. A few mechanics emerged from the hut and while one of them engaged Stan with some explanations, I could not help casting a searching look for our American ship. There was no mistaking her. The Liberator stood out like a giant amongst the row of Dakotas and Hudsons, obviously awaiting disposal after delivery from the States. Ignoring the cold drizzle and cutting January wind we walked twice under her wings and high tail, inspecting every inch of this brand new aircraft until the boarding steps were put into position. Inside, a mass of revelations. 'Hey, look at this, how about this and that!' Excited voices rang from all corners of the fuselage. Stan and I moved into the pilot's cockpit. Between two leather upholstered seats with padded arms rested a large ashtray, a most conspicuous item in the eyes of any RAF pilot.

'Can you imagine the court marshal if we lit a cigar in here?' I wondered aloud.

'Or even a cigarette,' added Stan.

Facing us was an almost mystifying instrument panel which, apart from the duplicated standard gauges, displayed two rows of some sixty identical switches with neat description beneath each, from NO. 1 STARTER to CABIN LIGHTS. The Bendix auto pilot like the rest of the electrical gear fascinated me especially after somewhat primitive hydraulic equivalents of the Wellington and I quickly realised why the size of Liberator's Pilot's Notes resembled the Old and New Testament put together. There was definitely a lot to learn and I spent the next week in and out of the aircraft memorising facts and figures according to the Notes. In the meantime, committed as I was to my exciting new job and despite of the necessary mental involvement, I did manage to put pen to paper at least twice, assuring my abandoned bride that everything at my end was going fine and that with a bit of luck I may be able soon to forward to her my new permanent address. Each letter, of course, was padded with millions of kisses and reassurances of eternal love. Thus, our military and private secrets remained intact.

Freezing February was now upon us as we commenced a short course in flying which consisted of few daylight hours of circuit work and one night cross-country. We were definitely ready for a change of climate when an operational order arrived authorising our departure. First point on route: Rabat Salle, Morocco.

The eight hour flight, mostly over the Atlantic, brought us to Africa early in the morning. We reported to Operations Control which like the rest of the base was run by the American Army Air

Force. There we learned that direct flights to Italy were prohibited because of stiff German resistance right across the southern flank and, until further notice, all aircraft are routed via Algiers and Tunis. That diversion took another three days to complete but eventually we did find our final destination which was Brindisi on the Adriatic coast. Any expectations of Italian blue skies quickly vaporised as we touched down in the pouring rain, sending clouds of spray across the waterlogged runway. The clever yet simple construction method for wartime airfields by laying Perforated Steel Planking (PSP) on runways and taxiways allowed aircraft operations to continue even when mud and water was a regular feature. However, my first experience of the noisy wheel clatter on landing and quite noticeable sinking feeling as our heavy Liberator finally ran out of speed was a little unnerving. The dispersal, except for aircraft hardstanding was a sea of mud. Our welcoming groundcrew, all wearing wellingtons and groundsheets, were almost apologetic for our inconvenience, and watched us plod, soaking wet, to a 3-tonner parked 50 yards away. We asked the driver how long this sort of weather is likely to last. 'Ee,' he sighs, 'that I don't know, but it must improve soon, it's been like this, on and off, since New Year.'

The narrow metalled road took us past barbed-wired fencing into the outskirts of Brindisi town. Where few white villas surrounded by greenery and tall palms looked quite out of place on a day like this. Still cursing our luck we entered the gates and driveway which led to another impressive Roman style house where we came to a halt. Between the two white marble columns of the entrance appeared several inquiring faces and we were hurried inside out of the rain. In the large hall, completely void of furnishings we met the backbone of our administration as well as some temporarily unemployed aircrew. Rather unusually within any squadron fraternity, our arrival created a good deal of excitement amongst those present, whose reaction seemed to indicate that any event in this building was a rare commodity. Greetings and inquiring voices echoed loudly between the tall, bare walls of the mansion while the warmth of our reception soon made us forget our cold wet hands and blue noses.

Peace and quiet returned with a sudden appearance of the Flight Commander. His name was Stefan Krol, Polish Air Force Major and

RAF Squadron Leader. After the introductions he led us to his office, one of the rooms down an empty corridor, followed closely by his Adjutant. He sat down behind a folding wooden table on the only chair in the room and inspected each one of us with a look of resignation.

'Gather around and relax. No one here sits on his dignity because we are all in the same lousy boat. I won't keep you long today but I must make it clear that our present spartan existence is no excuse for moaning or breakdown of discipline. You may have seen two Halifaxes on the pan. We are promised two more within a week or so and another Liberator at some time to complete the Flight's strength. After you have settled down, and I hope not later than tomorrow afternoon, Erik here,' he pointed at the rather surprised Adjutant, 'will tell you exactly when and where your first operational briefing will take place. In the meantime get to know the other crews, some of whom are already experts in bed construction, an essential task in houses with bare marble floors and no heating of any kind. We have already allocated three rooms in an empty villa nearby for all of your crew, haven't we Erik?'

The Adjutant, a young Flying Officer drew himself to attention with a quick reply, 'Yes, sir, we have.'

'Good luck, then, I'll see you at supper.'

We marched out and rejoined the boys in the hall. Guided by few willing hands we picked up our bags and set off in search of our residence. Fortunately the rain eased off to a few spots which restored a more cheerful atmosphere encouraged by the dry wit of one particularly helpful Varsovian.

'You see that wooden garden shed on the left? That's where we get our timber for bed making. There are still three walls standing so there should be more than enough planks for your boudoir. Blankets, like the rest of domestic stores, are in that house next to our Mess. The ruddy cooks keep their rations there. Note, there are no doors to that building and they don't need them. The two rooms inside are full of Argentinian corned beef from the last war and tinned potatoes from Ireland. After weeks of such extravagant diet who wants to nick any of it?'

'Do you mean there is nothing else to eat here?' I asked in disbelief

'Oh yes, there is. Twice a week they bring bread from the field bakery which tastes like sawdust, and on Sundays we get two slices of spam for lunch instead of corned beef.'

We laughed while he continued unpurturbed. 'Mind you, the spam is kept under lock and key in the steel cabinet with the snotty Adjutant's secrets! It's a good thing that the NAAFI manage to supply rations of spirits, a bottle of hooch per head per month, otherwise we could be arrested for complaining . . .'

We have now reached our destination and this jolly tour of enlightenment ended in the doorway. I spent that afternoon constructing my bed which would keep me four inches above the icy floor for the rest of my Italian adventure. To prove our introduction to life in Brindisi was not really funny I discovered within days that the monotony of our dietary existence was no joke. The cold water in the taps was unfit for drinking and not much use for laundering either. The warmth and comfort of our Liberator therefore made us keener than ever to get airborne and I even spent hours inside it chatting up the ground crew working on maintenance.

We commenced our operational task one week after arriving and immediately it became apparent that this tour would produce far greater challenge to navigation than enemy action. The vast area of our nightly operations stretched from Baltic in the north to the Alps and the wilderness of the Balkan mountains in the south. Because of the required precision in low flying at night with a radio altimeter as the only aid, apart from our eyes that is, dropping men and valuable material made these flights at least as exciting at times as my bombing trips over Germany. For administrative and security reasons all Drop Zones (DZs) had to be selected by people on the ground who often did not consider performance capability of aircraft involved. Some of our adventures, especially in Northern Italy or flying through the vicious resident thunderstorms of the Yugoslav mountains, brought us more than once too close to the gates of St Peter for comfort.

The one I am not likely to forget took place on 22nd March. At that time the Allies were still truly bogged down in the heavy fighting north of Naples and it was not our business to get mixed up in it, although, we often used the permanently active Anzio Beachhead as a bonus navigational aid. This stubbornly defended pocket of resistance was brightly illuminated by the heavy flak from both sides and was visible at night for miles. Although no one liked Dropping Zones in the Alps another trip did not appear to be any more demanding then the rest. At the briefing we learned that our task was to drop eight containers and two agents on a target close to the Swiss border which would be identified by a burning letter Y activated for 15 minutes starting at 0100 hours. The meticulous planning took a little longer than usual because of the heavy snow still present in the valley 7000 feet above sea level and any man dropped from 800 feet into a snowdrift even a short distance from the awaiting party would probably never see daylight again. I could not help but admire the bravery of these fellows who appeared like worn out civilians of a different age until a closer look at their eyes revealed hidden strengths of character and determination. Their camp near Bari 60 kilometers away was the main centre of underground activities and training but we never met them until minutes before take off. Our two 'passengers' arrived on time as usual and were guided to their seats in the back by the dispatchers. We took off 15 minutes later on a westerly heading and crossed the boot of Italy well to the south of Naples. Abeam Anzio, still pulsating with the most unfriendly multicoloured fireworks, we altered course northwards, aiming for the gap between Sardinia and Corsica on one side and the Italian mainland on the other. Soon, in total darkness and with some high cloud above one could only catch an occasional glimpse at the stars. We crossed the Genoese coast at 10000 feet and arrived over Lake Lugano, our turning point for the target, few minutes before 1 a.m. Ahead and to the right now appeared, as expected, the mighty snow clad mountainous ridge with its sinister white peaks well above our level. Eyes glued to the radio altimeter, we began descending towards the DZ in a valley 12 miles ahead. The dispatchers checked in to say that everything was ready for the drop. Four minutes before our estimated time to the target I watched the altimeter needle slowly approach 8000 feet. In the darkness outside one could almost sense the proximity of rocky cliffs and I felt my stomach tighten as I stared into the black void. Stan was first to see the faint flicker of burning letter Y. 'It's going to be tricky, we must try a first time approach,' his voice sounded shaky. 'Ready with the containers?'

'Ready, Skipper, doors open!'

'Wait for it . . . wait for it . . . let go!'

Seconds later a panting voice comes back, 'Containers gone and clear.' A steep turn to port and increased engine power brings us back towards the target but not on a reciprocal course. 'There is no wind in this hole,' says Stan, 'we can drop them on this run. Did you hear that lads?!'

'Yes, Skipper, they're ready.'

A slight sense of unease invaded my thoughts as we deviated from our original plan. No matter. Let's get on with it! I thought.

With only 2 minutes of fading letter Y left and now exactly at 800 feet above the target both agents exit through the door, their parachutes opening successfully as the connecting links to the static line go taut. There is an obviously relieved shout from the back: 'Thank Christ for that! They've gone.'

Just as we are about to turn away to starboard abrupt command from Stan comes like bolt from the blue. 'Hell, the mountains! Maximum boost: Through the gates, Jacek!'

I ram the four throttles through the wired up gates marked in red EMERGENCY ONLY and to my horror see snow covered rocks flash few feet past the starboard wing tip. I grab the control column and scream: 'Stan, look to the right!' We both haul back on our control columns with all our strengths and force the reluctant Liberator to climb steeply to the left, with the screaming Pratt and Whitney engines desperately trying to part company with the wing mountings. It takes only a few seconds for our heavy aircraft to run out of speed in an almost vertical climb. Unbelievably the imminent stall occurs just as the rocks vanish fleetingly beneath us and her nose plummets earthwards. Training takes over and we go into stall recovery. We plunge on down into the inky blackness with our speed increasing agonisingly slowly. Muscles tense as the seconds slip slowly by. We would scream again if we could see rocks in our path but our eyes, straining in horror, see nothing. Finally hope glimmers as we gain flying speed and come back to level flight under control. 'Good God, we lost 3000 feet and there was no ground in the bloody way! It's a miracle!' shouts Stan in relief.

'What was all that about?' frightened voices from the back sound justifiably full of anxiety. 'We've been thrown and battered against all parts of the fuselage.'

'Is that all,' barks Stan, regaining his composure, 'you're lucky to be alive. We're getting out of this bloody place as soon as we can.'

The roar of our double radial engines on maximum power amongst the alpine valleys must have sent echoes from Switzerland to Austria and back because as soon as we resumed normal flight artillery opened up as far south as one could see. We found our way out between well advertised defences of Turin and Milan heading for the peaceful starry skies of the Mediterranean. It was not until we were abeam Corsica that the subconcious after-shock suddenly took control of my body. For a few minutes cold sweat trickled down from my forehead and I had to force my clammy fingers to relax on the controls. I exchanged glances with Stan who was well aware of our brush with destiny. He was already on the second cup of coffee but still looked a bit white around the gills. He kept muttering about bastards who expect a Liberator to perform like a Hurricane.

It was a very relieved and subdued crew who finally walked away from the dispersal that morning.

Back in Brindisi life was beginning to get a little bit more comfortable with spring sunshine available for at least few hours every day, houses drying out and an unexpected improvement in our dietary monotony. While our stock of alcohol, regularly supplied by the NAAFI kept rising, our American friends on the opposite side of the airfield were putting on weight with such luxuries as butter, fresh eggs and steaks but had not a drop of whisky or rum to cheer up their souls. The imbalance of this situation became apparent immediately after two exchange visits between the squadrons and resulted in a completely illegal smuggling operation which put smiles on everybody's faces. The town of Brindisi was now in bounds and within a fortnight the few remaining Italians, obviously preferring dollars to Mussolini's lira greeted us with open arms and Marsala, a delightful southern wine with nasty after effects. How they managed to organise an instant operatic performance of surprising quality, with a five piece orchestra and tenors who would not disgrace Covent Garden, was a mystery to us all. Sadly, on some occasions the aircrew carried away by wine produced a choral finale which caused the weary inhabitants of Brindisi to close all shutters around the town square. As this was the only entertainment, apart from poker and bridge in the Mess, our visits there took place on the average once a week and I learned my first words of Italian when treating the musicians: 'Cinque Marsala per la orchestra.'

Way back in Blackpool Honey at last received my coded military address. It resulted in prompt arrival of detailed daily accounts of her existence plus heartfelt descriptions of longing for her beloved. Our field postal services, alas, managed to deliver mail from home only once or twice a week and at times I was obliged to answer as many as seven letters at once. I do not think, however, that this inconsistence made any difference in our blind desire for constant assurances of deep feelings for each other after just two weeks of marital bliss.

Three months after my arrival in Italy, this beautiful country still offered a few surprises including those provided by nature or ghosts of the Roman Empire, as described by our navigator, Kazik. The Americans and British were still stuck in Anzio and Monte Casino. Despite persistent powerful attacks from sea, land and air, they were unable to dislodge from the hills the mighty Tiger tanks equipped with the same quick firing 88s which had caused me a lot of anxiety over Germany. One more drop in the Alps seemed now quite a routine as we piled in into our Liberator after another careful operational planning. The weather forecast predicted cloud and precipitation from an almost stationary cold front north of Naples and proved to be correct. Before we reached the Genoese Bay skies cleared and the rest of our task went according to plan. Not a shot was fired and on the way back spirits were high. We entered the same patch of bad weather at 9000 feet before turning for home but this time icing and turbulence were much more in evidence. We did not see Anzio on this occasion. Either the nightly shooting match ended for a well deserved break or the cloud was too thick for any flash to penetrate to our level. On an estimated time worked out by Kazik I altered course south east for Brindisi. The sleet and snow stopped and the cloud appeared to thin out. Our signaler was in radio contact with the base now and having checked on the actual weather there I felt once again at ease.

Suddenly, weird things began to happen. At first I thought daylight was breaking through, then I realised sunrise was not due for at least two hours. The orange glow reflected by layers of cloud ahead grew steadily in intensity and soon all surroundings were pulsating unevenly in an eerie deep red light. Stan and I glanced at each other in bewilderment. 'Here, Kaz, come and take a look, I am turning right to avoid . . .' Before I could finish the sentence a tremendous force tossed the aircraft upwards. Seconds later it shuddered as if struck from above by a sledge hammer. Stan, ejected from his seat, hit the cockpit roof and dropped back with earphones round his knees while our flight engineer, who stood between us only a moment ago, disappeared to the rear in one uncontrolled dive. I desperately managed to hold onto the control column and watched an inferno of red and orange fire balls flash past the aircraft on all sides. Then, as suddenly as it began, turbulence ceased and the mysterious glow vanished leaving us in complete darkness. Somehow, without trying, we gained 500 feet!

Kazik emerged in a state of shock.

'You're too late,' says Stan holding on to his sore head, 'either some bastard invented a new weapon or we made bloody Anzio at last. Which is it?'

'Don't be silly,' our navigator's pride overcame the panic, 'that's impossible. You lads had better check your gear, there is a foul burning smell coming from somewhere.'

A thorough check of instruments and fuselage from one end to the other revealed no sign of fire or damage. Still, for the next half hour we sat on pins and needles, breathing in the slowly fading sulphuric odour, lost for any logical explanation. Although Air Traffic Control passed us visibility in excess of 10 miles and skies clear we found this, to put it mildly, hard to believe, as we were not able to distinguish the flickering goose neck flarepath until 1 mile on final approach. Landing was quite normal but as we alighted in the dispersal there was still a distinct lack of confidence in the confused explanations between us.

The Ground Chief with a powerful torch in his hand greeted us for the first time with abuse. 'What the hell have you done to my aeroplane. She is as full of shit as a Christmas goose! It will take weeks to get her right.'

Stan and I followed him on an external inspection. Our brand new Liberator was in a sad state. Its nose and all the leading edges were stripped of paint and the windscreens and turrets were opaque and caked with clinging dust which looked like ash.

'No wonder we couldn't see more than a mile ahead,' I thought aloud, 'but where did all this muck come from?'

We arrived for de-briefing and the intelligence officer met us at the door. 'Guess what chaps, just heard from Naples, Vesuvius erupted an hour ago, biggest bang since Pompei, towns and villages are being evacuated, pity you missed the fun.'

Kazik was first to respond. 'Ignore him,' he says, 'we were bloody lucky to be dead on track and survive!'

Of course, not all the operations from Brindisi were as nerve shattering as all that and my 18 trips to Poland, some of 14 hours duration, were particularly satisfying. Once over the Tatra mountains the whole countryside as far as the Baltic revealed one massive plain, split through the middle by the Vistula river and its tributaries. Large forests on either side and lakes and marshes to the north made a perfect shelter for the ever-growing resistance organisations, particularly the Home Army, with everyone geared up for action on a signal from London. However, from the beginning of 1944, it should have been more apparent with every passing day that all was not well with the inter-Allied relationships. Like the rest of my compatriots I still believed that Polish independence could never be in doubt since the principal reason for declaration of the World War II was the invasion of my country. Only in retrospect can I describe the hidden and devious decisions taken at the top which cruelly shattered my naive trust and optimism. This was due, I suppose, to the very nature of 1586 (SD) Flight operations. After all they did suggest full Allied support for self rule throughout Europe.

Significantly the sequence of events began with the untimely death of General Sikorski in a mysterious aircraft crash off Gibraltar the year before. Sikorski was the internationally much respected Polish Prime Minister in London who formed his cabinet from a selection of intellectual democrats based originally in Paris, most of whom opposed the military government in independent Poland of the thirties. With strong backing from Churchill, he negotiated the release of nearly quarter of a million Poles from the Siberian labour camps and was on his way back after inspecting the newly formed Middle East Brigade of enthusiastic conscripts. The results of any inquiry into his killing which was never publicised, probably for the fear of antagonising Stalin. From the beginning he must have hated any idea of a democratic Poland, and prepared his brief well, especially now, just before the forthcoming summit meetings with leaders of the West. It never occurred to me then that the glaring smiles and hand shakes of the world leaders can mean so little. My trust and naivety could not contemplate the thought that such a renowned philanthrope as Roosevelt could ever agree to hand over half of Europe from one ruthless dictator to another. The latter who was responsible for millions of his own countrymen's disappearance in the slave camps of Siberia, as well as cold blooded murders and assassinations which had shocked the world ever since Russian Revolution. Yet, Roosevelt preferred to ignore Churchill's warnings while his American advisors disregarded consequences of the Munich appeasement. Their immature judgement was eventually to plunge the humanity into 50 years of bloody conflicts and nerve-wracking brinkmanship. Unaware of this background in an imperfect world, my belief in fair play was encouraged by the continued outward British support for the Polish Government in London which was described by the Soviet propaganda, in the stereotype Communist phraseologies, as 'bourgeois reactionaries' or 'land owners out of touch with people'. At first such statements created more fun then worry, to half a million exiled Poles like myself who did not own an acre of land and had reacted only to the totalitarian dictatorship of the invaders. However, things must have been viewed more seriously by our leaders, especially Winston Churchill himself who decided to reinforce the Polish democratic structure in London from the ranks of the nationally supported underground movement in Poland itself.

Now, still in Italy, I was already coming to the end of my flying tour of 300 operational hours, happily counting the days to my reunion with Honey and a pint of English beer, when I was called in front of Squadron Leader Krol. By the formality of my introduction to him and his deputy, it was immediately clear that I was confronting

My Liberator – Helping with the maintenance

This was my crew, all of whom perished over Warsaw soon after this picture was taken. I am 3rd from the left.

a more serious matter then gambling the night before or keeping the Adjutant awake. The command 'Stand at ease, Blocki' did not improve my uneasiness as I waited for the reason of my presence there. After a nervous cough and some shuffling of the papers it finally came. 'You have been selected for a very special flight to Poland because of your experience on that route and because you have practically finished your tour here. The object of this exercise is to bring out some important people who are needed in London. You are going to be attached to a Dakota squadron in Bari as a second pilot, dispatcher and the translator for the whole of this operation. Not a word about this to anyone, and I mean ANYONE. You will go there by road this afternoon. Take all your kit with you, we don't know how long you'll be there. Any questions?'

'No sir, thank you sir.' I felt elated.

'Don't look so smug,' the Boss added, 'it may be tougher than you think. That's all Jacek,' he extended his hand, 'and good luck.'

I arrived in Bari at dusk. It seemed a similar airfield to ours except for the number and variety of aircraft packing every nook around its boundary. I was offloaded behind a double row of parked DC3s, Dakotas to the RAF, where I met Flight Lieutenant Jim O'Donovan, skipper for this clandestine operation. After few words together I learned that our trip was planned for the day after tomorrow and there was just enough time to meet the crew and acquaint myself with the inners of the most famous work horse of the war. I spent the best part of next day doing just that when the Squadron Duty Pilot arrived with a whispered message for Jim, confirming time of our briefing which was scheduled for six hours before take off. And so, on the 29th May 1944 I sat in a guarded Nissen hut, all eyes and ears, absorbing every detail of the briefing with nerve tingling anticipation. When a covered map was unveiled it became instantly clear that our destination was going to be even more exciting then anyone of us imagined. After the preliminaries one of the senior officers present began to explain the situation in a slow and precise manner.

'Welcome to the Operation Motyl 4.' He spelled each letter in turn. 'Blocki here will tell you it means "butterfly" in Polish. It involves landing in enemy occupied territory to rescue four individuals who are wanted back here in the West. As you can see from this map, the red arrow points at your target. It is an open field approximately 800 yards long with no significant obstructions on the approaches but it is surrounded by some shallow irrigation ditches. Its location is almost in the centre of a triangle formed by the rivers Vistula and San and Tatra mountains to the south. Even at night with a half moon on the wane you should not have much difficulty finding it. There will be a white letter T lit up from exactly half past midnight so work out your ETA carefully. In addition the boys on the ground will light three green lights at one end and three red lights at the other as soon as they hear the sound of your engines. You will have time for one circuit only to avoid exposing the exact location of the field to the Germans and there could be quite a lot of them not far away. These two lines,' he pointed to the map, 'indicate the latest state of play between the Russians and the slowly retreating Germans. This one, 25 miles to the east of your landing strip, indicates the extend of the Soviet advance and this one some twenty miles to the west is our estimated position of German's last serious attempt to stabilise the front line. We know that their eastern front Headquarters is already behind that line in Krakow. What could be good news is that neither of them will expect a third party between them in an area which is almost a no-man's land. The Met chaps don't expect any wind at that time of the night so it will be possible to take off in the opposite direction to make your exit as soon as your passengers are on board. All clear so far?' We nodded our heads while he emptied a glass of water. 'Who these people are even I don't know but they must be important and to make sure you bring the right guys, you, Blocki will identify them by the code name of this operation before they step into the aeroplane. By the way, you will be issued with a pistol but remember, two out of three previous attempts at these adventures have failed already because of the weather and unexpected German activity so don't try the impossible, even though this time it does look good. Take off eight o'clock and official night time does not start till 2100 hours. Oh, by the way, the best of British!'

After the briefing, during the supper and even on the way to the aircraft I do not remember any conversation between us apart from a few words from Jim reminding his crew of the time at least twice. In any case I found him a serious chap, not given to idle talk, something that one of his regular crew, a Scot, described to me as a South African characteristic. I must admit that our task ahead was not conducive to laughter and my own usual sense of humour was also absent during the preparations.

We took off in broad daylight hoping that long before we reached the Dalmatian coast line darkness would allow us some privacy. In fact in these latitudes dusk does not last too long and by the time we reached the Croatian high lands at 12000 feet night took over completely. A half moon, as predicted, appeared in the East and we caught a glimpse of the mighty Danube below. Again, tall Tatra mountains, still showing snow covered peaks, gave me an excellent fix and I assured the skipper next to me that all was going according to plan. We began descending for our destination soon after in an attempt to lose some 8000 feet as quickly as possible. Like magic a letter T presented itself dead on time followed by red and green lights just as we began a half orbit towards the final approach. After that things began to accelerate rapidly. As soon as our Dakota touched down and began to bounce on this unlikely runway I dashed towards the back door. The aircraft came to an abrupt halt quicker than I anticipated and three of us had to hurry to push it wide open. The cool night air of a Polish countryside with a powerful aroma of grass ready for haymaking burst into the fuselage propelled by the idling engines. I took one look into the darkness and jumped, revolver in my right hand. I landed in tall grass and crouched down. Slow revving engines were still too loud to hear any other sound though I could sense my heart pumping faster with every second as I waited impatiently. I took another deep whiff of the grass up to my chin. No wonder, I thought, we stopped so quickly. The take off will be interesting . . . The minute I spend there on the ground not knowing exactly what to expect seemed never ending. Suddenly, a huge shadow appeared from behind the aircraft's tail. A loud Polish voice abruptly broke the tension. 'Motyl czwarty?'

'Tak,' I replied, 'where are they?' Instead of replying he half turned and gave a short, shrill whistle. Three more shadows materialised instantly from nowhere. Luckily none of them were heavyweights and between four helping hands from the inside and two of us pushing from below we managed to bundle the three of them inside the plane. I turned to the remaining big fellow who extended his hands, gave me a mighty brotherly hug and breathed in my ear words I would remember to this day: 'Dziekujemy, dziekujemy z calego serca.' ('We thank you, thank you from the bottom of our hearts.')

'Are you not coming,' I asked surprised.

'Not me, the fourth man couldn't make it through the lines. Hop in before the Krouts smell a rat!'

I grabbed a handful of Polish grass and clambered back on board. There was no time to wave goodbye. A few hundred yards away machine gun fire announced a German presence and a criss cross pattern of tracers lit up the distant trees. I slammed the door shut and listened with relief to the roar of our engines. Our Dakota, however, was in no hurry to get airborne. As I jumped into my seat in the cockpit we were still crawling well short of take off speed. With tension mounting, the 800 yards of the field beneath us seemed long gone. Gripping panic at the thought of the undercarriage breaking in the invisible boundary ditch made me stare blindly ahead waiting for a miracle. It finally occured seconds after the three red lights disappeared underneath the roaring plane and we struggled into the air still in one piece.

'Christ Almighty, that was close,' puffed Jim in an uncharacteristic for him show of excitement and I pushed the clump of Polish hay deeper into my battledress pocket, protecting my memento for years to come.

We came back to Bari unmolested after a four hour flight to the most agitated welcome by intelligence officers I have witnessed to date. Our passengers were smartly whisked away while we spent two hours at the debriefing answering a barrage of questions. To my greatest surprise and satisfaction I was told that after a day or two of rest I was going back to England with the same crew and passengers and even in the same aircraft. There was just enough time to backpedal to Brindisi for clearance and farewells. With feelings of remorse I left my disappointed crew, who had already volunteered to extend their tour and half expected me to join them. Torn between loyalty and the irresistible need to return to my loving English family for a taste of normality, I voted for the latter even before my last unexpected deployment, but the decision was not easy. However, we managed a few drinks together and parted with many wishes of good fortune.

Three days later, still unaware of our passengers identity, I landed in Hendon, near London. My train journey from Euston to Blackpool kept me in a state of euphoria. I hoped Honey would not faint at the sight of her beloved appearing unexpectedly from nowhere. But, when I rung the doorbell at 10 o'clock that evening it was Mum who opened the door and nearly fainted after shouting on top of her voice: 'It's Jack! It's Jack!' The thunderous sound of foot steps on the staircase brought Honey into my arms.

'God, it is you, how did you do it?'

'Oh, nothing to it, I just had to win the war, that's all darling.'

With seven days of my idyllic leave remaining, a registered letter arrives creating more anxiety. In it is another railway warrant and an official letter which orders me to report to Headquarters Bomber Command High Wycombe wearing best blue. 'Why can't they leave you alone,' cries Honey but 'orders is orders' as the saying goes and I boarded the train for London as instructed. When we approached Euston station I saw my first experience of Hitler's last pangs of futile hatred in the shape of torn up rails and blown up homes, destroyed by the rockets nick-named Doodle Bugs. Eventually, I arrived, smartly dressed, driven into probably the most security minded complex of any wartime military establishment. In the large underground hall I am surrounded by very high ranking British officers, two Polish Generals and a number of important looking civilians and I feel distinctly uncomfortable. I recognise Jim O'Donovan and make my way towards him hoping for an explanation. He is as surprised as I am. 'We'll have to wait like all the others, we should soon find out.' Presently, the massive doors on our left open wide and reveal long, highly polished and silver bedecked tables arranged in a U-shaped pattern. White uniformed staff in the background add to the elegance of the occasion. We are invited to sit down as per a seating plan displayed at the entrance. I had to look more than once to make sure no one has made a mistake by placing a card with name of Flying Officer Blocki at the top table. When all the shuffling of feet and the search for right places ended there were at least half a dozen empty chairs still left in the very centre of top table while we waited for things to happen.

'Gentlemen, please be upstanding for the Foreign Minister, The Right Honorable Anthony Eden and his guests.' The deep voice from the doorway got me to my feet in amazement. I could not help but stare at the face a few feet away which I never expected to see in flesh, yet was so familiar from newsreels and newspapers. His arrival in the company of five individuals, I assumed to be senior Civil Servants, signalled the beginning of an official dinner which was another surprise. His after dinner speech which introduced the new Polish Government in London and my recognition of some of the faces that I had helped on the way to this historical event was equally unexpected. Finally, the words of praise addressed to the crew in this daring operation made my day and I felt really important for the first time in my life.

Later, fortified by a few glasses of wine I watched Jim O'Donovan being decorated by a Polish General with the highest decoration our country could bestow for bravery, the Virtuti Militari, an honour I had already achieved during my first operational tour. As the function began to warm up followed by more handshakes from VIP guests, the same General slapped my back and offered me any posting of my choice. Thinking this was an attempt at polite party talk I decided to be ambitious and suggested the world-wide Ferry Command Service based in Canada. 'I am sorry, sir,' I added, 'it is a most unlikely choice. Even our Chief of Staff couldn't pull that.'

'Well,' he replied, 'I have news for you, son, I am your Chief of Staff and I am going to have a try.'

CHAPTER 7

Peace At Any Price

On my return from High Wycombe I reported as instructed to the Polish Headquarters in Blackpool where I was granted two weeks leave and told to await news of my next posting. Together at last Honey and I spent one of those weeks in Torquay on our long overdue honeymoon without any interruptions. The familiar English summer of rain, drizzle and wind did not add to our enjoyment and the boarding house catering based on war time rationing made us long for Mum's cooking. The outside world lost its attractions and being together remained the number one priority. We managed to stay sweet and mellow even during the torturous train journey back home which took 18 hours including a beast of burden haul between two un-connected stations in Manchester in the days without taxis and limited public transport. We, like the rest of the public, became inured to such discomforts and austerity as the war taught us to be gratefal for small mercies. Meanwhile the struggle for supremacy or survival between the Super Powers continued unabated with the Russian bear in ascendance. Despite of the crippling losses in shipping and merchant seamen, the American and British aid in advanced technology and equipment delivered on the Arctic route to Murmansk and Archangelsk, must have played an important role in the Soviet recovery even though the Communist media preferred to omit any news of this kind. In Italy Monte Casino finally fell to the Carpathian Brigade which recorded yet another chapter of Polish selfless involvement in the fight for freedom. In southern England a mighty armada was assembling for the opening of the second front. Germany was on the brink of defeat and this was underlined by the

115

arrival of Stalin's war machine at the gates of Warsaw. It was high time for the significant Polish Home Army, directed from London, to show its muscle. The initial success of the uprising which liberated Warsaw and several towns behind the German lines took everyone by surprise, and Stalin, who halted his advance a few kilometers east of the Vistula, waited to see what reaction this would have on Hitler's still powerful army. The Western leadership's miscalculation became apparent when, after only a week of an impasse, two elite SS divisions smashed their way back towards Warsaw. It was obvious that instant assistance was needed and, since Stalin had no intention of intervening, a heroic air lift from Italy and England commenced with arms and ammunition for the beleaguered garrison in the city. Apart from my own 1586 Flight from Brindisi which was fully involved, many Lancasters of Bomber Command took part in these nightly operations flying to the limit of their operational range. Many of them failed to return, shot down in sight of the Russian troops who did nothing to assist. A month later in house to house fighting, the Germans retook the ruins of Warsaw and the Polish dream of independence was over. I found myself again at the crossroads of anger and frustration. I could never reconcile the slaughter of these brave patriots with the subsequent advance of the Soviet Army within a week into the dead city and I wonder to this day what excuse for his delayed action, if any, Stalin offered to Roosevelt and Churchill. More bad news arrived just as I was informed of my next posting to the Aircrew Rest Centre in Morecambe. Vitold, who had just returned from Italy told us that Stan Szostak and the whole of my crew left behind in Brindisi had been killed during the uprising, shot down over the centre of Warsaw. After that, I needed those three months in the Rest Centre.

At the end of summer, 1944, I walked many a mile at low tide across the exposed Morecambe Bay sands depressed and realising that only the survivors carry the burden of memories and plans for the future. Fortunately, after few weeks on my own, Honey was able to join me in the boarding house where I was billeted and this removed most of the nostalgic cobwebs as well as my sorrow which was an unusual emotion for me.

I began to enjoy organised games again, swimming in the pool, clay pigeon shooting and whatever else the Rest Centre had to offer. It was during one of our usual evening visits to the cinema that Honey shyly revealed that she was expecting a baby. What joy and excitement! Days began to flash by and our happiness was complete, for at least one month, that is.

I should not have doubted a word of the General, even if it was given at a merry reception. My posting to Canada materialised, as promised, at the end of November, a few days before I was due to leave Morecambe. At least Honey and I were allowed to spend our first wedding anniversary as well as Christmas Day together though only after some hectic preparations for the move which included a chase for a new passport and an American visa. After many hugs and kisses, I boarded yet another train at the start of a new, far away mission. This time I was offloaded in Greenock on the river Clyde where to my great surprise I realised I was to travel on the famous transatlantic liner Queen Mary. Stripped of all her luxuries but still looking mighty and proud she spent the whole war commuting between New York and Scotland, transferring thousands of troops in both directions. Her speed, like that of Aquitania and Queen Elizabeth, allowed her to sail unescorted on variable courses giving U-boats little chance of interception. I was to make many journeys on those ships returning from aircraft delivery flights in 1945 but nothing was as exciting as my first encounter with the Atlantic. After four days at sea I stood on the top deck observing every detail at the entrance to New York harbour while our majestic ship, surrounded by tugs and variety of small craft, made her way between Statue of Liberty and the skyscrapers surrounding the terminal. Three of my aircrew companions, who were on their first return trip via United States, could hardly wait to disembark after we were told that the next leg of our journey to Montreal by train from New York Central would not be until 1 a.m. Such timing gave us several free hours to feast on the sights and life within this massive cosmopolitan city. Armed with 40 dollars each, we did not waste much time getting our feet to work on the famous pavements feeling, quite wrongly, prosperous. After all, 40 dollars, the maximum allowed to us under existing currency exchange regulations, was equivalent to 10 pounds sterling and that sort of money in 1945 would keep a merrymaker in cigarettes and liquor for a month or more in the UK. In fact we would have been in the red after a second drink in a place called Belmont Plaza Hotel if it had not been for the patriotism inspired generosity of a portly senior citizen who was accompanied by two lovely and very expensive looking hostesses. The whole affair started after one wireless operator by the name of Jock Geary, who could not control his thirst any longer, persuaded the rest of us to investigate New York's high life, as portrayed daily in cinemas of the world. Encouraged by the scarcity of uniformed competition, in contrast to the streets of London, and hopeful of the interest the opposite sex would show to four young fliers, our natural male vanity looked forward to an exciting evening. Once Jock opened his mouth to an obliging taxi driver from Brooklyn, who referred to us as 'brave boys from across the pond,' the cabby was only too pleased to deliver us to one of the most expensive joints in the city, without mentioning the financial requirements needed in that establishment. Before even the scantily dressed usherette managed to collect our coats in the luxuriously furnished foyer, Jock found his way into an entrance under a sparkling image of a top hat where large but discretely lit up words read: NIGHT CLUB. Inside, we found a touch of Hollywood. A revolving crystal top hat big enough to accommodate 20 or more chairs around its brim and two barmen on the inside serving drinks from a lavish display of a mirrored hat ribbon behind them. Once again our uniforms seemed to have the desired effect and our first drinks were on the house. We were the only servicemen there and it was easy to deduct why some inquisitive customers at the tables soon joined us in conversation. Several drinks and a few battle scarred stories later, Jock's national pride insisted on reciprocating local kindness, his voice beginning to slur a little with excitement at being listened to by a gullible audience.

'Ah me lads, but have you ever tasted a real drink, like a wee dram of Scotch whisky?' He turned to the barman. 'I bet, you haven't got any, have you, Yankees?'

The penguin suited barman must have witnessed such bravado many times before and within seconds produced a freshly opened bottle of Vat 69. He expertly slung ice filled glasses in front of each customer. 'Will that be all, sir?'

Almost unnoticed a slip of paper arrived close to me. It was a bill for 86 dollars including taxes which sobered me up for a while as I pushed it in front of Jock. However, our gallant Scot was too busy to pay any attention to it and I was too happy to care, listening to the mellow tinkling on the piano next to me. With two hours left before our train's departure, and the bottle of Scotch nearly empty, the afore-mentioned portly gentleman arrived with his party. Obviously well primed by alcohol, his face glowing pink, he wavered unsteadily at the entrance, took one look in our direction, grabbed both of his shapely partners and with a beaming smile headed straight for us. 'Come on girls, meet the heroes!' His shout was the last thing I remembered clearly although I did vaguely recollect being pushed into a taxi and having difficulty in climbing into the bunk of a sleeping car.

I woke up looking at a very dark face of a steward who patiently tried to explain that breakfast will cease in 15 minutes because Montreal was on the horizon. It was a pity that my self inflicted brain injury from the previous night prevented me from appreciating the comforts and luxury of the American railway system, but as I sat at the table laden with cereals, eggs, bacon, toast and steaming cups of coffee, I was really sorry that after years of austerity and rationing in England my appetite could not do justice to the amount of food provided. My fellow sufferers presented an even more depressing picture and Jock was put in a doghouse for the rest of our journey. As the train slowed down and the first city buildings began to appear past the diner's window I suddenly remembered the bill.

'Hey chaps,' I asked, 'How did we square the money?'

'We didn't,' says Jock in a weak voice, 'Pinky paid for everything, just as well, it came to nearly two hundred smackers and that was only our share . . .'

On the first visit, my stay in Dorval, Montreal's international airport and wartime principal air transit base, was a short one. After three days I was in another train enjoying a magnificent winter scene of the wild Canadian country side which brought back the nostalgic memories of my early skiing adventures in the snow clad forests of Poland. I was on my way to North Bay, Ontario, home of 313 Ferry Training Unit, 45 Group Transport Command. Behind this grand title was one landing strip surrounded by many wooden huts of various sizes, the largest being a communal Mess where the aircrew spent most of the free time available. Almost completely cut off from civilisation one could really concentrate on the course of advanced flying technology. This included my first insight into the theory of flight which made me think hard about how lucky I had been to survive so far with such limited knowledge. On my very first trip in a B25, a Mitchell to the RAF, a very calm instructor feathered the port engine on take off while we appeared to be still firmly on the snow covered runway. He then climbed dead ahead to the circuit height, turned down wind, restarted the engine and commented: 'See how easy it is when you know what is involved. All you need is speed.'

Six weeks later I passed the course with an above average assessment and a first pilot's qualification entered in my log book for three more multi-engine types. But my enthusiasm for the job in hand was again blunted by the news from Europe. This confirmed that the West were planning to recognise Stalin's puppet regime in Poland with all the implications of a police state directed by the KGB from Moscow. It was also the first time I realised how deep the Communist propaganda and naivety of the general public affected Western opinion. After the wasted, thoroughly dedicated and unselfish efforts in the cause of freedom by myself and the sacrifice of both my crews killed in action, this news filled my last few days in North Bay with anguish and bitterness. At the farewell party I sat deep in thought with a Coke in front of me while my British course mates celebrated in an aura of beer assisted happiness. Naturally, it was not very long before my odd, dead pan appearance attracted their attention.

'Come on Jack,' for that is how the British solved Polish pronunciation problem, 'come on lad, there is nothing that a pint of this lousy beer won't cure. The war is nearly over and we are all going home soon.'

'Lucky you,' I tried to be not too serious, 'you don't think I'll be going back, do you?'

'Oh, don't be so bloody morbid. Uncle Joe will look after you, don't worry . . . isn't it better than being a slave to the capitalist land owners you left behind?'

At this point I did not know what to say so I lost my temper instead. 'You must be either bloody stupid or been reading Pravda if you believe all this Communist rubbish. Are you telling me that the quarter of a million Poles in England alone, all in uniform, who fought like hell to get their country back, and survived, did it to escape from their land owners?! They know bloody well what to expect from your Uncle Joe: Ten years in Siberia for befriending such as you and learning the joys of freedom!'

A moment of silence followed and it was obvious to me that none of them heard this kind of view which was not broadcast to the public even in the western media while the brief love affair with the smiling Russian dictator continued. Finally, one young Flight Lieutenant gathered his thoughts and with equal passion challenged me to a duel.

'And what do you want us to do about it? Start another war? You're crazy!'

'Forget it,' I said with prophetic inspiration, 'you will not understand what sort of a bloody mess this world will end up in until the war is over.'

I walked out hating myself, feeling friendless and abandoned. I sat on the end of my bed buried in self pity. Suddenly, one of my father's pearls of wisdom flashed back from years ago: 'Life is like a baby's nightie,' he would say, 'it is short and full of shit, no matter how many times you try to change it, son.' Five minutes later I got up and rejoined the party.

My first flight from Dorval was in a C47 which took me via Goose Bay, Reykjavik in Iceland, to Prestwick, Scotland's principal airport. This was the standard northern route for medium range aircraft from Canada and the United States while Liberators and Lancasters were able to fly directly from Gander, New Foundland across the Atlantic. Each time an aircraft was delivered to Prestwick there were at least three days available before arrangements could be completed for the return to Canada so I was only too pleased to catch the first available train to Blackpool with a bag full of tropical fruit such as pineapples and bananas, not seen on this side of the Atlantic for years, which were delivered to my expectant Honey with tender thoughts. On the way back sailing soon lost most of its original appeal, mainly due to the conversion of liners like Queen Elizabeth into hospital ships. The sobering experience of being in the company of maimed, or badly injured GIs on the way home created during each journey a vivid picture of war's horrors and emphasised the cost of the Allied crossing into France. Most moving of all was an attempt by one of the nurses to explain to a blind and legless soldier the scene outside, as the Statue of Liberty came into sight at the end of another tragic homecoming.

And how could I forget the Indian steamer called Ranji . . . an old lady that should have been retired after World War One.

It all started with a wrong forecast of our baby's arrival, which according to Honey's medics should have happened at the end of April. I had to make a desperate effort to persuade my Commanding Officer to grant me the delivery of the last B25 scheduled for the UK so as to coincide with our offspring's arrival. Normally, the limited range of this fast fighter bomber did not make it a very attractive proposition to pilots of 45 Group, especially as it involved an additional stop for refuelling in a ghastly place called Bluey West 1. To land on that strip, which was cut out of the perma frost and granite in a deep fjord in Greenland with 4000 foot high vertical cliffs on three sides, required weather conditions of unlimited cloud base and visibility, not the common occurrence in a birth place of many Atlantic depressions. But, this was nearly the end of the war in Europe and the numbers of aircraft delivered to UK were already being greatly reduced making home visits a rarity. After the usual, weather caused delays, I landed in Prestwick on 25th April and did not waste much time getting home full of nervous anticipation. Not only was the stork late but the baby failed to materialise at all, even by the end of my week's leave. Anxious and sad I returned to Greenock on 1st May 1945 and the same evening boarded SS Ranji with 5 other passengers. She was minute in comparison with the Queens, yet the two berth cabin seemed more cosy. My first experience of Far Eastern smells, which originated in the galley and oozed out throughout this freighter made me wince once or twice but the pounding and vibration of the ancient engine took a little longer to get used to. In the morning I found myself bouncing up and down on my bunk and decided to have a look outside. A stiff

Atlantic breeze made the small ship dip and roll at peculiar angles making me hold on grimly to the rusty rails. Ahead, I could distinguish the shapes of several other vessels and it was obvious that we were part of a convoy. I did not see my fellow passengers in the tiny diner either at breakfast or at any meal for the first three days but I must admit that I had found little enthusiasm myself for the incessant diet of curries which were predictably too easy to digest. The monotony of this journey was only interrupted twice by severe gales south of Greenland when the fear of capsising was only comparable to the fear of being left on our own at the mercy of U-boats. All the other ships in the convoy could not wait for one lame duck and had raced ahead of us long before the storms. However, a friendly destroyer did manage to find us on the 10th day and, miraculously after weaving between the icebergs for another 4 days, we finally arrived in Halifax, Nova Scotia.

After an additional 36 hours on the slowest train in Canada I arrived in my flat in Montreal, mentally exhausted, dying for the news from home. To my horror, the French Canadian landlady whose English was mixture of both languages expressed surprise at my arrival saying she understood that I had left for good and had redirected my mail back to the post office! It took me two agonising hours in the Central Post Office to trace a telegram dated 5th May which read: CONGRATULATIONS STOP BEAUTIFUL BOUNCING BOY ARRIVED TODAY STOP LOVE HONEY. I do not remember what I shouted but it must have been loud. Most of the people in the office turned towards me as I ran outside. The rest of that day I spent in our aircrew dive called the Tick Tock on St Cathrine street, sharing the news with all that were present and getting awfully drunk. Meanwhile, unknown to me, my poor family on the other side of the atlantic had to face the consequences of my landlady's misunderstanding. The day after our proud grandad dispatched the news of my son's birth his telegram was duly returned with two words added: ADDRESSEE MISSING. Honey who was still in the nursing home after the tough delivery of a son weighing nine pounds, was as shattered as Jim who brought the bad news. Hours of tears and agony followed until initial panic was overcome and it was decided to contact the Polish Headquarters in Blackpool for the official version of the tragedy. But it was another wait till the following morning which left the whole family mentally drained and my darling wife in a state of shock before a telephone message from the Air Ministry was received in Blackpool. It simply said that Flying Officer Blocki is not listed as missing, and to their knowledge, is still in transit to Canada. Even so, the effect of this blunder ruined all the deserved happiness on such occasions, especially that the stork chose to arrive on the VE Day. Unfortunately for me, I had to wait until the following September before I could see my son for the first time, after I flew home one of the last Lancasters manufactured in Canada.

The end of World War 2 was, of course, universally accepted as the greatest triumph imaginable and generated euphoria which echoed for months. However, one small but significant part of Allied force to which I belonged, unanimously held an opposite view. It was not easy for the Polish nation and its fighting forces to accept the domination of a foreign power which was based on complete state control and the denial of religion to a population totally committed to Roman Catholicism. As far as I was concerned, I could not even contemplate the loss of personal freedoms which I had learnt to respect so much within the British society. The emotional let down feeling experienced by thousands of Polish troops now in Britain became an exercise in self pity and depression which, at times, I could not avoid sharing on my return from Canada.

With only a handful of Poles willing to return to their native land, the British Government was confronted by a humanitarian problem on a massive scale. They decided to compensate their loyal allies by a generous resettlement programme of two years duration conducted under the auspices of the Polish Resettlement Corps. Early in 1946, while stationed in Dunholme Lodge in Lincolnshire, one of the units of the Corps, I was called in by the British Commander.

'Have you any immediate plans, Blocki?' he asked.

I hesitated for a moment surprised at the sudden interest in my welfare. 'Well, not really, sir. My brother and I are still discussing our future but it looks like forestry in Canada or Argentina. Both countries are offering pretty good terms for private enterprise just now but we need much more gen before we decide.'

'Oh that's good. We need a chap like you. Your English is well above the average and while you are waiting, how would you like to improve it further by obtaining Cambridge Proficiency Certificate?'

'That would be useful,' I retorted as I began to wonder where this line of conversation was leading.

'In that case you can pack your bags tomorrow because I have a job for you which will satisfy not only your personal needs but also the patriotic duty of every Pole to help his own kin.' He looked at me with an inquiring eye and continued: 'You must be aware of the plight of your fellow countrymen from the Middle East who escaped from Russian prisons to join the Polish Forces there. Well, they are here now in East Anglia. Unfortunately 90 percent of the blighters don't speak a word of English. First, you will attend an English instructor's course in Cambridge where they certificate people. Then you will go to one of the PRC camps to introduce the language to your compatriots. All this should not interfere with your plans for retirement because there will be the usual leave and holiday allowance and we shall remain your parent station wherever you are.'

I arrived in Cambridge three days later and attended lectures for the following six weeks. Apart from introducing the technique of teaching, the course boosted my confidence when I realised that most of the 800 thousand words in the Oxford dictionary were ignored by the English themselves and were certainly not a requirement necessary at my tutorial level. But it was nice to add another language proficiency, this time on paper, and I was anxious to put it to good use. The PRC camp Riddlesworth in Suffolk was a wartime British Army holding unit which now accommodated several hundred Polish soldiers, some with families. It was miles from anywhere but it had a charming atmosphere of unspoiled countryside which was enhanced by majestic oaks and birches, colourful carpets of spring flowers and the sounds of pheasants and wood pigeons from behind every tree. Even the camouflaged Nissen huts below, connected by overgrown footpaths, fitted in with nature's wonderland and no one at first sight would have guessed there was a thriving human community within.

Only a few days after my arrival I assembled a blackboard in the largest of the huts used as a dining hall and, with two lessons each morning and two in the afternoons began to teach the most willing and attentive students any teacher would wish to have. The Polish Camp Commandant hearing that I left my wife and baby son behind, kindly furnished half of the hut next to him with camp beds, a rather worn carpet, table and chairs and offered it as accommodation for the whole of my family. I was delighted if not a little apprehensive about Honey's reaction to austerity of the place but it was all compensated in the end by so much friendly assistance, that from the moment she arrived with our little Michael, she had nothing but praise. This was our first married quarter at the time when a married accompanied posting for most Servicemen was an unheard of luxury.

Months went by, some of my students made remarkable progress and those with technical skills such as cooks and drivers already began to drift into the post war civilian life. In fact, most of my compatriots within the Polish Resettlement Corps who had attended civilian training courses during that year were busy now sorting out their future, be it in UK or anywhere in the West. From correspondence with my friends in Canada I knew that there were some vacancies with Trans-Canadian airlines and I could start there as a second pilot on Yorks, which was an airliner converted from the Lancaster bomber. A lucrative salary of 800 dollars a month was very tempting but I still toyed with the dream of a private, import-export company, an opportunity encouraged by the South American Governments, according to my brother, Rafal, who made several visits to the Argentinean Embassy in London. That idea went bust after my own interview ended there with a bare faced request for a substantial bribe by a senior official, 'to smooth the beaurocratic process,' as he put it.

I returned to Dunholm Lodge in 1947, now at the ripe age of 25 and just in time to witness the great international panic created by Stalin's blockade of Berlin. To add to the world's misery Mr Fuchs, our trusted nuclear-physicist, decided that a cold war was better than no war and handed over the atom bomb secrets to the Soviet Union. The short lived honeymoon with the Soviets, as anyone could have predicted, was over. With all the hopes of everlasting peace, disarmament and coexistence gone I should not have been surprised to receive an official letter inviting me to attend the Royal Air Force Commissioning Board, but I was! The prospect of a peace time commission never entered my head while millions of Servicemen were being dispensed with in the post war euphoria. Still disbelieving any chance of acceptance, I turned up in the same St Johns Wood offices I had visited way back in 1940. This time, however, the corridors were nearly empty and in the reception room I was the only uniformed fellow amongst the twelve candidates. Had I any confidence left, the interview itself would have shattered it anyway, so I treated the conversation and questions thrown at me with a nonchalant resignation of a man not likely to succeed. In any case the three gentlemen behind the desk, seemed to know more about my past from the detailed records in front of them, than I could possibly remember. As usual, after an interview I was asked to wait outside. Three hours later, all twelve of us were still in the reception room comparing the devious questions and some silly answers which we had just gone through when one of the interviewers appeared in the doorway. 'Flight Lieutenant Blocki?' I stood up holding my breath. 'You are to report for a medical on the floor below. The rest of you may collect the railway warrants from the secretary here for your return home.'

I hardly noticed the congratulations and hand shakes of the departing candidates, nor do I remember the details of another tough aircrew medical except that the examining doctor asked me to step up and down a chair for the second time disbelieving my pulse rate, something I eventually learned to live with. Later, when the secretary officially told me that I had passed my interview as well as the medical examination my elation was complete.

My arrival home in the early hours of the next day must have awakened most of our neighbours with screams of delight from Honey and general excitement from the Nadins' household while my head seemed to swell larger than any doorway in sight.

The following month I received a very formal letter confirming my Commission in the rank of a Flight Lieutenant in His Majesty's Royal Air Force with instructions to report to Topcliffe in Yorkshire. My Service number was to be 500059 which meant I was the 59th officer commissioned after the war. After that, my pride and dedication to the Service was to remain high for many years to come.

CHAPTER 8

British By Choice

Three months after arriving in RAF Topcliffe, home of the No 1 Air Navigation School, I had a pretty good idea what was expected of me, particularly as a newly appointed Flight Commander. My commitment to the Service prevented me from concentrating on personal issues but in retrospect I must admit that while in the No 1 ANS I did earn the 45 pound monthly salary more than any subsequent pay increases. The post war RAF policy of believing that good pilots are automatically highly qualified administrators and leaders of men left me in a hollow state of underconfidence as I started to learn the responsibilities of my job from square one.

Apart from some 20 aircrew, I was responsible for at least 30 NCOs and airmen of the ground crew who were engaged in the 24 hour servicing of the eight aeroplanes in my Flight. This involved me in matters of continuation training, discipline and the important aspect of morale maintenance. On occasional days off I spent hours writing personal assessments trying to be as fair as Solomon himself and from this I learned enough about human nature to become a social worker. Every Wednesday morning I paraded my Flight on the taxi-way opposite the hangars with the rest of the Station. This was done regardless of the weather which can be most depressing during the winter in Yorkshire. There was equally no excuse for not attending open air sporting activities the same afternoon and it was my responsibility to ensure that everyone under my command enjoyed it. Wednesday was also the only week day without night flying and instead, every officer had to attend a dining-in function, one of the rare occasions when I was able to meet the Station Commander or his Wing Commanders. Since all of us in Topcliffe were in the same boat no one expected much sympathy about personal family affairs and the lack of married quarters and resulting separation was accepted as a standard hardship. The nagging accommodation problem throughout the British Isles, especially in the proximity of military bases, meant a constant search for anything remotely suitable for habitation by the thousands of newly married couples who pined for togetherness with the advent of peace. As the winter of 1949 announced its presence with a heavy snow fall I had my opportunity at last. Despite the usual panic created by what should have been a well organised snow clearing plan, flying had to cease and I found myself with a little time to spare. As I walked towards Thirsk, the market town close to our airfield boundary I found an old man pinning a sign to the gates of an ancient looking country house advertising: ROOM TO RENT. This cold and damp bed sitter with a portable paraffin cooker gave us one of our rare experiences of independent family life. Despite the comfort and welcome available in our parents home in Blackpool, having Honey and my only son so close, outweighed most of the other problems which confronted me then, and many times later, during my Service years.

Slowly but surely I began to grow feathers of experience and a professional approach to flying and administration. My Polish origin remained as always the subject of wisecracks until my English fellow officers, unable or unwilling to deal with any foreign languages, abbreviated my name to Jack, which saved hours of explaining why an addition of one letter E made such a difference in pronunciation. Thus, I stayed Jack Blocki, alias Black Jockey, as one wit would have it. Aircrew are like that!

At the end of 1949, No. 1 ANS moved to Hullavington with all its Ansons and Wellingtons and, due to ever increasing international tension, the pressure of work was doubled. The production line of pilots and navigators reached almost a war time level and new types of aircraft began to fill the skies all over again. In our case, the acquisition of a Valetta class room, enabled us, at any one time, to take up to twelve young navigator trainees into the air with supervising instructors. This practical experience, often in thick cloud and severe turbulence, was considered the quickest and most accurate method of finding out whether an individual adapted, when airborne, to map reading, plotting, astro-navigation and coped if necessary with air sickness. The results often amazed me. Day or night, on any cross-country at the turning points, I could be confronted by errors of 50 miles or more and wondered how we survived during the war without such advanced training methods. But now, I was possessor of a Master Green Instrument Rating. This pilot's qualification allowed me to fly in any weather conditions, except when diverted by operational authority, and that was the reason, I suppose, for my guiding these fellows in the first place.

To everyone's surprise, my tour of duty in Hullavigton ended abruptly after I was offered a post of OC 23 Group VIP Communication Flight in Swinderby at the age of 29. It opened a new world of experience. An experience not so much in keeping the aircraft's ashtrays clean and neatly arranging the window curtains, as observing the often humorous behaviour of the high ranking public figures in private circumstances. Alas, half way through my most enjoyable flying with a dignified reception at almost every airfield or airport, the powers that be decided that it was time to modernise the Royal Air Force and no aircrew over the age of 30 would be able to enter operational squadrons of Bomber or Fighter Command. It was hard to swallow the feeling of obsolescence at my age. In common with many other victims of this short lived policy I decided on completion of my 3 year tour in Swinderby during which I ran my own miniature airline without much interference, to apply for a ground specialisation. Due to the shortages in certain ground branches my application must have been eagerly accepted for I was posted within weeks to Shawbury on an air traffic course.

I arrived in Full Sutton as a high intensity qualified Air Traffic Controller two days after completing the course and soon learned how to control panic as well as aeroplanes. The experiments of the RAF into forming an all-weather air force at the advent of the jet age without proper aerodrome recovery aids proved a very expensive exercise. It mainly affected pilot training in the secondary flying schools such as Driffield and Full Sutton in East Yorkshire. The unpredictability of the weather on the North Sea coast, with sea fog or low stratus rolling inland winter or summer at short notice, meant that it was probably the least suitable part of Britain for Meteor conversion. Meteor, the first operational jet of the Royal Air Force, was severely handicapped by an endurance of only 45 minutes. The recovery to base of up to 20 of them in deteriorating weather with only primitive direction finders as an aid was hair raising on occasions. We were lucky in Full Sutton but Driffield much nearer to the coast suffered probably the heaviest peace time loss of life and aircraft on one station anywhere. Unfortunately, the continued treatment of air crew as an expendable commodity since the days of my stern leader, Bomber Harris who was affectionately known to the few survivors of Bomber Command as 'Butcher' Harris, continued as a necessary evil of our defence policy until, the famous West Raynham disaster in the early 60s. The loss of nearly a complete Wing of jet fighters on a major exercise over East Anglia, all trapped by widespread thick fog, finally proved too costly and after that a distinct change in attitude became apparent throughout the Service.

My private life continued in a haphazard way with accommodation and schooling the principal responsibilities. Our social life had moments of pleasant existence in company of the colleagues and their wives at the Officers Mess functions and local hostelries. However, home entertaining was generally impossible in the one or two rooms of the farmyards, converted war time schools and lofts of cottages which were the only housing available within twelve miles of Full Sutton. Honey became a responsible Service wife, known again to everyone as Hilda. Like all the other suffering wives during the days of austerity she was not always happy but was always ready to cheer up in the female company while sharing life's ups and downs. Our son, Michael, now a 7 year old and already showing signs of disorientation after several school changes, became our number one priority. Maybe because of the debt I owed my own parents who, at considerable cost, released me into the demanding new world with an acceptable standard of education, I decided, against stiff opposition from the rest of the family, to make a similar sacrifice for our offspring. Boarding schools were still considered by majority of the English as an upper crust fancy which had heartless and even cruel connotations and this led me for the first time into some very strongly developed class opinions. To make sure that the boy would never be far away from the family circle Hilda and I decided to try the well established Arnold School in Blackpool. As I soon discovered, this minor public school with a high reputation throughout Lancashire was not an easy place for one's offspring to enter. After an interview with the Headmaster I found that the school was as much interested in the parent's curriculum vitae as it was in the son's. Michael was accepted into the junior school from the age of eight as a boarder and, as a by-product, I felt I was elevated to the middle classes without any experience of class consciousness. The price was high. Apart from Hilda's tears during those days, the annual fees of nearly £300 without any assistance from the Service reduced our income by a third.

In October 1954, one year after Michael entered the portals of Arnold School I was aboard Her Majesty's troopship Empire Clyde bound for Singapore and Malaya, another hot spot created by the Soviet's ever expanding worldly subversion. Although Hilda accompanied me in the first class cabin with all the pre-war luxuries it entailed, the 28 day voyage via Suez, Aden and Colombo was marred by the constant sorrow of a mother deprived of her only son and I began to think I had committed a crime. Some months later both of us realised that with hardly any educational facilities in a war torn country our decision was right. Meeting an intelligent, well mannered, teenage boy, who accompanied his parents throughout the father's 3 year tour in Malaya but who could hardly read or write, did help to change Hilda's attitude. On the other hand, one snappy remark at a party by another wife: 'I could never leave my child behind!' brought more tears for a day or two.

Our arrival on Singapore island was, to say the least, exciting. With the usual shortage of married quarters we were accommodated on the south eastern shore in a boarding house called Katong Grange. It was run in the Victorian colonial style by an ancient but well preserved madam. White clad servants serving tiffins or teas on the lawn under the coconut palms and formal dress in the evenings was the order of the day. Not far away was the social centre of the British community in Singapore. Equally snooty it consisted of an Olympic size swimming pool, restaurant, ballroom, casino and two bars, all superbly looked after by a multitude of Chinese staff. In contrast, life on the other side of the muddy, stinking Singapore river was an entirely different world. After our first visit there, mainly to discover hitherto unknown secrets of the Orient, Hilda never ventured near it without a perfumed handkerchief, even after our dull European senses developed a passion for Chinese, Malayan and Indian cuisine. Of course, I was not allowed to waste time on swimming, croquet or bridge, the latter being a passionate hobby of our hostess, and I found myself instantly in the middle of the operations from RAF Tengah, home of three fighter and one bomber squadrons, part of the Kuala Lumpur Group on the mainland. To spend a day or two with Hilda I had to acquire my own transport in the shape of an old Wolsley limousine and then negotiate the 15 mile journey home through the diabolical traffic of many oriental road users determined to commit suicide. To add to the political upheavals throughout the Far East, the decision by the British Government, a year before our arrival, to return a young Dutch girl to her parents in Europe, created spontaneous anti-White riots in the whole of Malaya. The girl who was left behind after the Japanese invasion was married to a Muslim at the age of ten and the religious fanatics exploited this event to spread killing, burning and looting on the streets of all the cities in the region. Our safety in Singapore, already partially established with the arrival of a strong Ghurka contingent, was still the subject of careful procedures and during my first few months at Tengah a Thompson machine gun accompanied me on each journey through the restless city. I also kept it under my pillow at night though with the loaded magazine removed for safety and kept in a dresser to give Hilda an additional sense of security.

In the meantime, the jungle warfare across the Straits of Johore against the increasing number of well trained terrorists infiltrating from China and Russia via Thailand was a tough nut to crack. The dense, almost impenetrable tropical jungle which covers this part of the world proved to be not only a perfect shelter but also an ideal base from which to attack and terrorise the local population and our protecting Forces. Round the clock bombing and strafing of the reported hideouts by Australian Lincolns as well as our Venoms and Hornets was soaked up without trace and, initially, did more damage to monkeys and parrots than to the invisible enemy. Ground operations proved equally ineffective as penetration of the jungle in a maximum effort averaged only two to three miles a day. Torrential tropical downpours, heat, mosquitoes, and millions of other insect biters did not help either and one had to admire the grit and stamina of soldiers bred in the cool climate of the British Isles, emerging after days in the jungle with heavy packs on their shoulders. New tactics were devised and implemented but even so, by the end of 1955 two thirds of Malayan peninsula was far from being a safe place to live or travel through. It took best part of that year to establish several landing pads for helicopters in the middle of the jungle to enable a rapid deployment of troops into the reported trouble spots. This was done by cutting down two or three giant trees, some as high as 150 feet and burning them on the spot to prevent new rapid growth beneath the permanent green canopy of the forest. My first helicopter descent into one of these cutouts was like going down in the lift of a multistorey building into a dark cellar. The six soldiers with full battle gear disembarked quickly and I watched them disappear into the foliage. Poor devils! It would take them three weeks to get to the nearest British outpost even if there was no contact with the enemy.

On one occasion my liaison duties with the Army provided a much brighter side to this nagging war due to nature's unpredictability. When the State of Johore became a centre of terrorist activities it was decided to carry out a major cleaning operation based on the Kluang air strip some 50 miles north of Singapore. My job was to take a convoy of two fire vehicles, a portable air traffic caravan and two escorting Land Rovers to open the strip for the use of troop carrying Valletas and helicopters from Kuala Lumpur. On the bumpy, narrow twisting road through the jungle, it took the best part of a day to reach our destination where I was greeted by Wing Commander Le Cheminon, the man in charge of the operation. After a briefing, I inspected the small airfield, found no problems there, but the Sergeant in charge of the fire section reported two bullet holes in the bowser which must have come from our 'friends' in the trees. No one heard any shots on the way and the mystery remained unsolved. I bedded down with my contingent in one of the three Nissen huts on the domestic site expecting the first aircraft to arrive at the crack of dawn. Instead, just after midnight the Monsoon arrived.

Torrential rain accompanied by the constant roar of thunder created such noise on the corrugated roof that sleep was quite impossible and after an hour I braved the weather to see what was happening outside. Drenched to the skin within seconds I watched the reflected flashes of lightning on a lake which only yesterday was a grass landing strip. I ran across to the hut next door and found the Wing Commander and our Signals Officer busy drying out two field telephones on the soaked table. From the brief conversation punctuated by some swearing I deduced that both lines were out of action and so was the contact with the world outside.

I ventured an unlikely solution: 'I could try my VHF transmitter, Tengah might still be within ground-to-ground range despite the weather.'

'Well, what are you waiting for. We have to postpone everything, unless someone finds a few flying boats. Let me know as soon as you make contact.'

I dashed outside and headed for the Air Traffic caravan. There, two radio mechanics, who had found a quieter place to sleep, jumped up from the floor as they were sprinkled by the water running down my legs.

'Come on lads, we have to open for business!' I shouted. 'Get me Tengah approach frequency.'

Half an hour later a faint crackly voice acknowledged my transmission. 'You're strength one, go ahead, go ahead Kluang . . .'

'Important message for Operations Kuala Lumpur . . . please relay . . . POSTPONE OPERATION RAINDROP, I say again, POSTPONE OPERATION RAINDROP . . . airfield flooded.' I paused here to give them time to copy. 'Did you get that?' Despite my doubts Tengah acknowledged the message without a hint of humour.

The rain continued in heavy bursts for nine days, and although the whole operation was canceled on the second morning after our arrival in Kluang, we were literally stuck in the mud for the whole period with no hope of recovery.

Just as we were getting used to the continuous noise of the downpour for two nights running, a brief appearance of the sun on the third day created in the huts an atmosphere of a sauna steam baths and I ventured outside in search of fresh air. What I found, however, proved to be far more conducive to the restoration of morale and waning enthusiasm although, at first, I had to subdue my personal feelings in front of other ranks. While checking my mobile air traffic control systems, pitifully resting in one foot of water, two empty beer bottles floating nearby attracted my attention and I tackled a happy looking radio mechanic, who was lounging inside, about my discovery.

'Oh that,' he says, 'it's nothing, sir, we'll soon get rid of them when the water subsides, there may be a few more around here . . .'

Surprised, I interrupted his explanation suggesting that the bottles were full to start with. He nodded his head and smiled, 'Yes, sir, full to the top!'

'And where on earth did you find them?'

'Oh, we didn't, sir, it was Flight Lieutenant Evans who found the beer. There is a barrackful of it in the Army camp down the road.'

I plodded through the lake outside towards the Nissen hut designated as a temporary operations room which was now condemned to stagnation. As I entered the door water droplets the size of walnuts descended from heavens once more.

'Come in, come in Blocki,' greeted my Wing Commander sitting by the table next to Evans with half empty bottles of beer between them. 'Here, grab a chair, guess what Taff found this morning . . . try this for size . . .' He leaned down and lifted a bottle from a crate underneath the table and pushed it in front of me. His tall, distinguished looking figure, slightly worse for wear, turned to Evans. 'Come on Taff, what happened to that bishop's daughter in the end?'

It took me only two bottles of the powerful Malayan Tiger beer to start appreciating the type of humour I found on arrival in that ops room. From under the Welshman's handlebar, ginger moustache poured out a series of funny stories which must have originated in one of the Cardiff rugby clubs. Red faced, perspiration running down his face his final offering was topical.

'Listen now, this is just right for this bloody place,' he continues uninterrupted by his tiring audience, 'it happened in a jungle just like this. Steaming hot, only cicadas rubbing their legs together and all other animal resting exhausted. An old rogue elephant stands leaning on a giant tree, panting. A little snake slithers through the undergrowth and stops in front of the tusker.

'Hey there,' he says, 'how about a game?'

'Push off,' replies half asleep elephant.

'Oh, be a sport, I am bored,' persists the snake.

'Push off, before I trample on you.'

'Don't be like that, Elephant, in this game you don't have to do anything, just say "surprise" if I surprise you or "snookered" if I don't. It can't be easier than that.' Tired of listening the elephant finally agreed.

'Ready?' says the snake.

He coils himself tight, springs into the elephant's trunk and comes out of his bottom. 'How was that?' asks the snake.

'Surprise,' grunts the elephant.

The little viper hesitates for a moment then jumps into the elephant's bottom and comes out of his trunk.

'How was that?'

'Surprise.'

'Great,' revels the snake as he springs again up the elephant's trunk.

The tusker swings the trunk back, sticks it in his arse and says, 'snookered, you little bastard!'

After that we had to retire but the jokes continued for the rest of our detachment in Kluang each time another crate of beer was delivered.

Back in Singapore the long working hours in the hot and humid climate were compensated by our social life and the many friends with whom we shared the luxurious facilities of the Singapore Swimming Club or mouth watering eating places. The latter, in their abundance, stretched from the primitive stalls of Bedok Corner under the palm bedecked coastline to the elegant Chinese restaurants in the city. One person mainly responsible for our assimilation with the Orient was my old pal from the days of Hullavington. His chequered career in the Royal Air Force deserved a principal place amongst the outstanding characters ever commissioned in peace time. Flight Lieutenant Roy Chandler, known as Chan, one of the many staff pilots in that busy school for navigators, was renowned for his wit and an ability to enjoy any party including games after our weekly dining-in nights. But he disappeared one day from the station without trace and without a single good-bye. Finding him on Singapore island four years later, still full of fun, appetite and a willingness to help anyone in need of enjoyment, meant an instant table for four, Peking Duck and several beers.

While our wives engaged in a typical conversation of female interests I could not wait to hear what the mystery of Chan's sudden departure was all about.

'So, what the hell are you doing here, is it something secret?'

'Don't be bloody silly,' he said with a broad grin on his face, 'I am running the target towing Flight in Seletar in other words: Brigands with condoms.'

'And how long have you been here?'

'Nearly three years.'

'And before?'

Chan takes a goodly swig at his beer, has a sheepish look around the tables next to ours and leans nearer towards me. 'Oh, that's a long story.' His voice drops a tone lower. 'Do you remember that horrid crash in fog, when one of our Wellingtons exploded on take off after hitting the hangar full of Spitfires?'

I nodded my head. 'How could I forget? Twenty bodies and the biggest fireworks since the war. I was diverted to Valley that night.'

'Well, I was second in line for take off behind the poor bastards. All crash vehicles were fighting the blaze and we were recalled to the dispersal. One could hardly see next taxi light . . . you would think they would cancel flying for the rest of the night, but no, we were told to wait in the crew room until crash facilities are back in place. I had a bit of a cold anyway and decided to see the Doc who sent me to bed. Next Wednesday, as usual, I turn up at the Dining-in Night. The ante room is packed and we stand like penguins, sipping sherry and waiting for the meal. In walks Barry, that thick headed Squadron Commander of mine, remember him?' Chan did not wait for an answer and continued: 'He made his way towards me and in front of everyone says in the loud voice, "Still got the shits Chandler?" Well, I ask you . . . big as he was I lose my cool and reply: 'Would you like to step outside, sir, and repeat that?' Chan took another gulp and put his glass down. 'We walk out into the corridor and Barry continues his innuendo on the theme of cowardice. I get really mad and land my best punch on his face . . . his nose pours with blood and I walk out of the Mess.'

'Bloody hell,' I could not control my curiosity, 'what happened after that?'

'What do you think, Jack? Next morning I am marched in between two Squadron Leaders in front of the Station Master expecting to be court marshalled and instead, within a week I am on a plane for Car Nicobar, nine months unaccompanied.'

'That's not so bad,' I said, 'tropical island in the Indian Ocean and little to do . . .'

'That was the problem,' Chan replies, 'I got in a spot of bother because of this excess of boredom. One supply run a month and two Vallettas for refuelling in all that time can drive you nuts! Only one of these Vallettas had to come a few days after I organised a beach party for my lads and the natives. We used both fire vehicles on the island to carry the goodies as well as the men to a beach two miles away. Unfortunately, after an unexpected downpour neither of the vehicles could be extracted from the wet sand and we had blown our fire cover. It could have been another court marshal, but everyone kept quiet about it while the Vallettas came and went. After a month of hard labour we finally managed to dig out the heavy bowser while our only Land Rover vaguely performed the standby duties. In the end, for services rendered, I suppose,' here Chan lifted his head and smiled, 'I was finally posted to a vacant accompanied post in Seletar as a Flight Commander.'

After this confession I looked at Chan as a cat with only seven lives left but two months after meeting him in Singapore I also felt that without characters like him the Royal Air Force would have been a much duller Service.

It was then that one more coup-de-grace ended his Service career at 100 feet over the dispersal of the Tengah based 60 Squadron. The day before, he had returned from a routine mission of an air to air firing exercise with two bullet holes in his Brigand. To remind the over-enthusiastic fighter boys that their job was to hit the target he was towing and not pushing, Chan loaded the Brigand with toilet rolls, flew next morning across to Tengah, swooped over the dispersal and showered his vengeance on the neatly parked Venoms of 60

Squadron. With a little bit of research he might have got away with it, but on that very day 60 Squadron were being inspected by the Air Officer Commanding from Kuala Lumpur and the traditional parade was in full swing when the toilet rolls came down!

It so happened, that a few months before the Air Ministry decided what to do with the surplus aircrew and enticed many of them to take premature retirement with a grant of £5000 in cash. This was a substantial amount of money in 1956 and it became known as a Golden Bowler. Chan, when confronted by a court marshal, decided to accept the generous offer which in the long run probably eased the tax payers' burden.

The 'bombing' of the 60 Squadron may not have contributed much to the Malayan war effort but all of us at Tengah felt somewhat uplifted by the sheer audacity of an inventive, yet misguided mind. Certainly, 60 Squadron pilots thought this was fun and made a change from the daily strafing of the unseen enemy. Later that year though, they were to be congratulated with all the other Tengah squadrons for a decisive mission which helped to end terrorism on the whole peninsula and eventually enabled Malaya to gain independence from the British rule. Like in all tricky operations, an element of luck played its part after years of disappointments.

Before dawn, three fighter squadrons followed the Australian Lincoln bombers to the primary target which was confidently recommended by an intelligence report from the mainland. Alas, on arrival the whole Force was confronted by a solid blanket of jungle fog and low cloud making recognition of terrain quite impossible. As instructed, all aircraft headed for the secondary target and despite the obvious disappointment blasted it to smithereens.

Weeks went by before an Army platoon reached the bombed area. Under the massive canopy of the Flame-of-the-Forest trees they found the shattered remains of several atap huts and 59 bodies. Further investigation revealed that the bodies belonged to the top cadre of the Malayan underground terrorist organization which gathered together on very few occasions and in one lucky strike they had all been destroyed.

The overall tension and all out effort of the past two years was coming to an end and I even found time for a flying refresher on a

Vampire jet with the 60 Squadron instructor. Hilda's moment of happiness came early in the summer with arrival of our son from England on his only visit allowed during our tour. The poor lad contracted a dose of gyppy tummy in transit through Karachi's infamous staging post called Minwallah's Grand Hotel Malir. It took couple of weeks to get rid of it, but when I suggested an extension of his holiday, Michael said he would rather go back on time because he was promised the captaincy of the junior rugby team at the start of the next term. Now, Hilda and I felt completely free of any remaining guilt complex for the first time. To add to our satisfaction Michael passed his 11 Plus exams, considered then a stepping stone to higher education, and freed us from the burden of school fees.

Our return home from Singapore was unexpectedly delayed until April 1957 by the blocking of the Suez canal and the subsequent French and British skirmish with Nasser. Yearning for any semblance of stability and family life, so often disturbed by the Service demands, we put all our savings into a deposit on a house in a residential area of Blackpool, a few hundred yards from Arnold School. Michael became a day boy in the senior school to the delight of Mum who could not wait to offload all the pent up care and attention on her only son. Of course, that meant myself becoming a long distance commuter, although for the next 5 years I was lucky to be posted within 80 miles of home plus another 2 years in Preston Air Traffic Control Centre on Emergency Service which, apart from the job, was a blessing.

During all that time, the Royal Air Force like the other two Services, suffered a never ending cycle of contraction and expansion with each international upheaval which often caused a good deal of personal hardships. This made me feel grateful for selecting a specialised ground branch not involved in redundancies. I began to cast my eyes into the future and wondered who would employ me now in civvy street as a pilot at the age of forty when I was considered too old 10 years earlier. However, my commission was extended in the General Duties branch to the age of 55 and I was able to venture into the more exciting thoughts of not needing to work after retirement from the Service.

CHAPTER 9

The Final Itch

With the passing years I found that despite the security of a permanent commission in the Royal Air Force I had an evergrowing anxiety about life on the other side of the fence, namely: 'civvie street'. The ability to live and work with people who share similar interests within the same enviroment is not what the civilian world generally has on offer. Even to this day, the frequent moves each Serviceman is obliged to carry out, as well as the occasional months of separation, encourage families to get acquainted with new faces almost immediately on their arrival. Hilda and I knew well in advance that, after my retirement the loss of such companionship would require quite a lot of readjustment and the need for self reliance in whatever pleasures or hardships that came our way. Of course, the umbrella of financial security enabled us to seek in advance a more interesting and outward existence although I must admit that some of my ideas were only carried by one vote with one abstention. Still, that is how democracy works anyway . . . Already at the age of 45 and with 10 years to go before my retirement I did not relish starting any job for some new civilian boss and because of my overall fitness began to consider a number of more adventurous options. We had already invested in a mobile caravette and spent several summer holidays with our son and his pals touring as far as Italy to the south and Scottish Grampians to the north. The luxury of having a real live in home on wheels enabled us to visit a most satisfying selection of destinations with many stops in beautiful places far from the standard tourist attractions. For the family, none of these were more pleasurable than the Rhine valley or the Swiss lakes but I was already bitten by another bug. In the early sixties, during yet another tour in Yorkshire at RAF Leeming, our aptly named Devonette took us several times down to Devon and Cornwall in search of new pastures and a warmer climate. The discovery of the romantically associated old harbours and creeks, with their historical background of fighting ships, smuggling and piracy, sent my imagination to the days of boyhood and dreams of sea voyages and discovery. As the saying goes, 'the difference between men and boys is the cost of their toys.' Unashamedly, I set out to prove it by trying to convince my home loving and delightfully feminine spouse that there are better things in life than growing roses. At first it was just a dream but after a visit to Hartwell yacht builders in Plymouth, Hilda began to weaken, which allowed my ambitions to flourish. Although the cost of buying a 32 foot Golden Hind, made of teak and mahogany, was at that time quite unrealistic in our financial situation, I persisted in visiting the yard to scrounge a few sailing trips and watching the master craftsmen at work. To Hilda's satisfaction my leave allowance on the very active station was strictly limited and the emergence of other more serious personal problems forced me to divert my interests elsewhere, at least for a year or two.

Of course, our freedom of movement enhanced by our caravette, did not permit even a thought of travelling to the other side of the Iron Curtain though the news of my family in Poland was getting progressively more depressing. After a large injection of cash by me to the Polish authorities in London, dear mother managed to obtain the rare permit to visit us in England 5 years after father's sudden death in 1954. There was no possibility of her staying with us permanently and now she was almost unable to travel because of her deteriorating heart condition. The main reason for mother's need to return to Poland was her right to the two bedroom flat in Luban, previously a German provincial town in Silesia, but now annexed by Poland. This right was granted to her as the widow of an ex-prisoner of war, who was now reconciled with the Communist regime, despite father's high rank in the pre-war Poland. The flat soon became the family's retreat when Mum took under her wings our homeless Auntie Zofia with her husband. Had she absconded to the West the consequences would have been obvious. During those long years of separation I was able to help my dear mother with parcels and money but our regular correspondence, strictly censored behind the Iron Curtain, was no substitute for personal contact with her son. My brother Rafal, now fighting horrendous inflation in the far away Argentina, was certainly not in any way capable of assistance. Finally in 1968 I received a confidential letter from mother's doctor in Luban stating that her illness has reached a terminal stage and she was not expected to last more than six months. That was a big blow and, at first, I felt helpless. I knew that no British Serviceman would be allowed to penetrate the Iron Curtain for personal reasons but in desperation I decided to make some inquiries. To my surprise and gratitude I found that there were no real hard hearts in the Royal Air Force or even in MI6 when I finally arrived there for a briefing. It was made clear to me that whilst I would not be allowed to travel through East Germany, either by land or even by air, there was another option and fortunately our caravette solved the problem. A carefully planned route would take us via Nuremberg to the Chech border leaving us only 200 miles to go to the Polish frontier post. The necessary visa and transit formalities were left to me to arrange but I was told that I must be frank about my status and reasons for this journey. A sobering comment came from a Group Captain in our intelligence cell in London: 'You are going behind the Iron Curtain of your own free will. If for any reason you get detained on route or in Poland we may not be able to help. Remember, they are lords upon themselves . . .'

A month later, for that is how long it took to complete the paper work, Hilda, myself and our Devonette, loaded with the essentials as well as some luxuries from the 'capitalist' world, boarded a North Sea ferry for the Continent. There was no question of my loyal spouse staying behind especially as the recommendation by my official advisors was that a husband and wife team would portray to any suspicious Communist official a more genuine picture of an innocent family visit.

The outward journey was uneventful and we were surprised at the general welcome in Chechoslovakia with people waving and cheering at the sight of the small Union Jack Hilda had attached to

145

the side mirror. In Prague the streets were full of excited people and at first I thought that there must a major sporting event taking place, until a man ran towards us pointing to a copy of the London Times in his hand. It was June 1968 and the Chechs like many other oppressed people under the Russian boot were getting ready for a taste of freedom. We smiled and waved back but kept moving because our one day transit visa stated we had to cross into Poland before dark. In fact, I drove towards the red and white barrier of the Polish frontier check post with only an hour of daylight left. We were immediately surrounded by guards bearing Kalashnikovs who, without saying a word, waved us out of the caravette in a most unfriendly manner. Our British passports and visas were taken to the guard house while Hilda clung to me outside with three Kalashnikovs pointing in our direction. Her pale face and shivering hands made me stifle my own fear and I managed few words of comfort.

'There, there, darling,' I whispered, 'they probably haven't seen tourists before.'

An agonising half an hour later a Corporal arrived. He rummaged through the caravette and disappeared back into the offices ignoring us completely. Another 15 minutes passed before he emerged again with our documents, handed them over and barked in Polish: 'You're clear to go.' But, as the barrier was lifted I heard him give instructions to the remaining guards in Russian and wondered what sort of an outfit was really looking after the security of Poland. We moved out smartly and as I drove away I could not help looking into the back mirror to see if we were being followed. At the same time I attempted to concentrate on the signposts in the fast fading light with not a soul in sight to help with the directions. Just then, Hilda, who was still on the edge of her seat looking nervously in all directions, uttered her first words on the Polish soil.

'That was some welcome,' she sighed.

We arrived finally in Luban that same evening to an absolute contrast of wholehearted greetings and tears of joy. Mother, who according to Auntie Zofia had spent most of the previous weeks in bed or in the chair, suddenly acquired a new lease on life and had to be restrained from accelerating up and down the two storey staircase. My first aim was to visit father's grave and this we did on the second day where I spent a long time in thought amongst the neatly laid fresh flowers caringly arranged by Mum. The character of Luban itself did not impress me as a part of Poland which I remembered as a youth and the general outward drabness could only be described by the American definition of Dullsville. Still, someone had declared that it would be Polish from now on and there was not a single German to be seen within the Teutonic streets and architecture. The highlight of our stay there was a surprisng invitation to a party, from the Area Garrison Commander, a youngish looking Colonel and his elegant wife. Mother said this is one invitation we couldn't refuse and reminded me that all people of that rank are proven Communists. The party which in a typical continental fashion, started early in the afternoon, was obviously organised with an intention to impress such a long lost compatriot as myself. Wines and vodka of the highest quality were supplemented by appetizing caviar and smoked ham. The gathering of uniformed officers, a few dark suited civilians and their expensively dressed wives mingling on an open patio in the warm June sunshine could have occurred in any five star hotel in the West. After the alcohol began to take its effect, the Colonel, who spoke a little English, was most willing to listen to Hilda's complaint about our reception at the frontier.

'How do you expect anyone to visit this beautiful country if you greet people with the machine guns?' she asked with a genuine expression of disappointment.

The Colonel, taken aback by the audacity of probably the first dissatisfied person he had seen within his command, apologised to her for the rest of the evening. Later, when even his Polish began to sound somewhat laborious he insisted on personally showing me the way to the toilet along the narrow corridor. Once out of sight of the others he put his arm around me, his hot breath close to my ear. 'Sluchaj, Panie Jacku . . . what do you think . . . we are not doing too badly considering the bastards on our backs, what?'

'No,' I said, 'you are doing very well.'

'Here, my friend, I want you to have something to remind me by.' The Colonel unpinned one of the badges on his uniform. On the red and white enameled background were imprinted words 'POLSKA ARMIA LUDOWA' {Polish People's Army). 'Keep it,' he insisted.

147

Next morning Aunt Zofia got up at 5 o'clock and came back three hours later.

'What on earth were you doing at this ghastly time?' I asked.

'My dear,' she replied, 'if you don't join the queue at the only bakery in town before six you don't get any bread. They run out of everything in two hours.'

'So much for equality in this Communist paradise,' I sighed aloud.

The abundance of the agricultural riches of pre-war Poland were not to be seen anywhere on our visit in 1968 and I witnessed for the first time the reality of life there. Certainly, it was vastly different from the hypocritical slogans which exploited so cleverly and cruelly the naivety of under-privileged people elsewhere and especially in the newly emerging countries. In contrast, no ordinary people on this side of the Iron Curtain seemed proud of the definitions like 'People's Army' or 'People's Democratic Republic' which were deliberately misused by the self imposed absolute rulers and whose interpretation of democracy must have made the ancient Greeks turn in their graves. A week after our arrival I encountered another extra-ordinary example of disloyalty to the regime which had been imposed by a foreign power when returning from Poznan after a motoring excursion into part of the country I had known since before the war. Trying to find an alternative route back to Luban I asked a group of young people on a street corner, who seemed to be delighted at the sight of our Union Jack, if there was a more scenic road in that direction.

'Oh yes,' says one with a cheeky smile, 'if you take the next turn right after 10 kilometers, you will find a brand new road through one of our beautiful forests. You might enjoy it.'

Unfortunately I took his advice and found the road. It was straight and new as he said, but after 50 miles with no traffic to be seen, I found myself passing between rows and rows of stationary Russian tanks. Sheepishly we observed their leather helmeted crews busily prancing in and out of the undergrowth. I asked Hilda to remove our little flag but even so, the presence of our camera on the back seat made our hearts race for the whole of the next 40 miles, not even daring to glance at the red star markings of the Russian armour.

'What would they have done to us if they realised who we were,' asked a relieved Hilda after the forest saga ended in the open fields of Silesia.

'I don't know, but I don't think they would have offered me a job in the Red Air Force,' I suggested.

Two days later, after another tearful parting, we arrived back at the same border check point and were told once again to leave the caravette. This time, however, we were politely invited to an office where a Polish Army Major presented Hilda with a bouquet of red and white carnations and I received a large bottle of cherry vodka.

'Compliments of my Colonel,' said the Major, 'and he wishes you a pleasant journey home.' He clicked his heels and saluted as we thanked him on the way out.

'That's better,' announced Hilda back in her seat, 'it takes a woman to sort out this world.'

And I could not disagree.

We arrived back in England without any further excitement and I reported to the MI6 cell in London to tell them that all had gone well except for the amassment of the Russian tanks on the way south.

'Oh, that is nothing unusual down there,' said one official in pin striped trousers, 'their troops are almost on constant manoeuvres these days.'

Nothing unusual! Well, the next day the Russians invaded Chechoslovakia and Dubcek's dream of independence was dead. For me though the great sense of achievement in the whole affair was mother's miraculous improvement which extended her life by another two years.

Alas, Hilda's parents had died within 15 months of each other a little earlier and the sombre thought of becoming the remnants of a past generation made me even more aware how short one's presence is on this earth and the need to use it to the fullest in the time available. My long Service and associated life of ups and downs was an excellent preparation for things to come but, of course, that was nothing I considered of value after my flying days had ended. The rapid progress in the world of aviation demanded not only a change in aircraft design but also, rightly or wrongly, brand new selection methods for aircrew. A few hiccups like the incomprehensible political decision to scrap TSR2, the most advanced aircraft of its day, may have delayed the progress for a year or two and cost the British technology dearly, but bits and pieces which gradually emerged later still made predominantly computerised flight a reality. With it came the need for pilots and navigators with a university degree at a cost in the region of five million pounds each, even before they were proficient enough to join an operational squadron. However, while at Leeming, which in the late sixties, was still a Jet Provost station I discovered that the scholastic mind of some of the students did not fit the three dimensional aptitude necessary for flying an aeroplane. These failures in training proved a very expensive waste which could never have happened in my early years. I remember laughing at the sarcastic comment of one instructor, while discussing a particular failure of the new concept in aircrew selection.

'Jack here must remember the 1914–18 war,' he says to the amusement of all present, 'the only requirement to become a pilot over the Somme was to do as he was told, keep his mouth shut and his bowels open.'

After the laughter died down I chipped in: 'And how do you know that?'

'My grandad told me!'

More laughter.

As years flew by I began to convince myself more and more that slowing down from 600 knots, the fastest I ever flew, to 6 knots at sea with no airways or fog bound runways, would be the answer in my later years. Still fit as a fiddle at the age of 48 I often distressed my spouse, by aiming at any harbour for an outing, although my favourite haunt was always Plymouth, the birthplace of all the Golden Hinds. This attraction must have been subconciously creeping under my skull since I sailed my first dinghy made from two Hornet wing tanks in the Johore Straits or Albacores in the heat of Tobruk harbour, and now, the sight of an open sea even on a cold and windy day off the Northumberland coast held a magnet I could not resist. The little offshore sailing which I was able to enjoy then whetted my appetite even further, and after my posting in 1970 to Ouston, home of a University Air Squadron, I was also able to dig in into the theory of seamanship.

150

Our students were working for their degrees in the local universities and flying at Ouston took place mostly at the weekends. I eventually learned from these fellows that a number of part-time courses were available in the South Shields Marine College, internationally famous since the days of Captain Cook. Among the subjects available were navigation, chartwork and seamanship. I visited the college, found everyone most helpful, paid the fee of £8, and made arrangements to attend classes on Mondays and Tuesdays when the airfield was closed.

Thus in March 1972, I started commuting thirty miles to South Shields, attending lectures, and collecting a substantial amount of homework for the remainder of the week. My classmates were a mixture of merchantmen, fishermen and amateurs, all trying to improve their seafaring status. Some of the revelations by experienced crews of the Icelandic fishing fleet were not only of value but left me with even greater respect for the sea.

After a few weeks my tutor, a keen young Captain, suggested that I should try for a yacht master's ticket. He must have been impressed by my standard of navigation and chartwork, normally the toughest hurdle in the professional progress of first and second mates. The hard grind of the remaining four subjects was conveniently ignored and I agreed.

Back home our lounge was converted into a lecture room in which, for six months, our leisure would be sacrificed for a life of scholastic swotting. Throughout this period my Hilda was simply wonderful. She ensured that any moments of weakness on my part were a passing fancy, proved herself a patient teacher, an examiner, and was my strongest morale booster. While I quoted collision regulations or described buoyage systems, she would check the relevant sources with care and point out any errors. She learned how to send Morse by light, and, her small energetic self performed a miracle with semaphore flags. Neither of us knew or had used this method of signalling before.

My homework became a matter of routine. Nautical books and notes filled all spare corners. Half-spliced, whipped, or knotted rope was stowed away each evening, ready for the next practice.

I began to make progress. In May I sat my first examination in

Newcastle and passed navigation and chartwork with flying colours. Finals came in September and I was controlled by the Ancient Mariner himself. After the thorough grilling for two hours that made me wish I had never started, the old Captain, who had spent half a century at sea, sensed my practical inexperience even though the 100 per cent pass required in subjects such as Sea Rules, Buoyage Systems and Tidal Prognosis was obtained. In the end, however, he raised his bushy eyebrows, smiled and pronounced me a Qualified Yacht Master. As I uttered an astonished thank you, he shook my hand and said, 'You my not be a complete sailor yet, but with your enthusiasm I am sure you will become one soon.'

Just after my examination, prompted by one more venture into the freezing North Sea off Whitby, I decided to apply for my last posting to Cyprus and when this was granted my ambitious plans began to materialise. Our move into a married quarter at RAF Nicosia in the heart of Cyprus in April 1973 heralded a cycle of events which no one could forecast. My job was once more connected with an emergency cell, this time within the Nicosia Air Traffic Control Centre which was responsible for the safety of flying in the whole of the Eastern Mediterranean. Our building was situated on the domestic site 200 yards from the only runway of Nicosia International Airport. There I discovered why it was that the RAF who took over such task in an independent country which was quite capable of looking after its own business. It all revolved around the innate upheaval between the relatively new State of Israel and the Arabs. A particularly ugly series of airline highjackings was beginning to create an international outcry and I found myself in the middle of some nerve wracking situations. None were worse than the highjack of a Lufthansa Jumbo with nearly 300 passengers on board which lasted three days and nights and which in the end made a cool and collected German pilot, who had a pistol to his head throughout this incident, finally sound like a man ready to commit suicide. Neither Cyprus or any other country would accept the aircraft but after two refuelling stops in Lebanon, Libya allowed the plane in after the Captain threatened to crash the Jumbo into the sea. Listening to such tense voices and passing the messages to the highest authorities who were engaged in political games with human lives at stake made me often frustrated and angry.

'What a bloody job on my last tour!' I kept bitching to myself

But, when it was all over and I lay next to Hilda on the beautiful unspoiled Kyrenia beach, the events of previous night soon vaporised from my mind and the picture of a Bermudian sloop replaced all thoughts, before the brain drifted into the land of nod.

The big adventure could not wait any longer and, after I secured a loan against my terminal gratuity, I ordered a new Golden Hind in Plymouth. It took nine months to build her in our absence, while my almost daily correspondence with Terry Erskine, the new boat yard owner, kept me on my tenterhooks until the following January when Terry finally confirmed the date of completion in 30 days time.

Despite the scepticism of family and friends I planned to sail her to Cyprus myself and obtained special permission from the Air Officer Commanding to be allowed six weeks leave, the total yearly entitlement of an officer, to do so. I had discounted the French canals as too slow to negotiate and raised many an eyebrow of the more experienced skippers by announcing that I was routing via Biscay and Gibraltar. But the chilling thought of wintry passage without a properly trained crew persisted and had to be answered. The problem of an experienced crew was simply solved by their non-availability, and I had decided to rely on the self steering and Hilda's loyalty and ingenuity.

I have always been a keen observer of the weather and climatic patterns. I noticed that towards the end of February a high pressure system often established its reign over Scandinavia and brought forth cold easterlies over Britain and the sea areas to the south. This wind direction, of course, would be ideal for my schemes, but we had to prepare for a freezing session. We had ordered the warmest, lightest, and most expensive weatherproofs in the business, and Hilda knitted incessantly. Ironically, an assortment of mittens, balaclavas and jumpers came off this production line in the heat of Cyprus. During that hot summer I spent most of my spare time trying to improve on my practical sailing experience with the Near East Forces Cruising Association based in Akrotiri and made considerable progress considering the leisurely character of that organisation.

Our 32 foot Bermudian sloop was named Smoo-Cher after our

153

faithful boxer bitch who departed to the kennel in the sky at the age of 10. The extremely difficult selection of one yacht out of the dozens of types available on the market had been carefully considered by both of us over the years of waiting and while Hilda was enthusing over the spaciousness and internal elegance of the old fashioned timbers I was considering her performance as an ocean going vessel. The fact that the previous 134 Golden Hinds proved themselves seaworthy all over the world was encouraging but what swayed me most was that 100 of them which were sold to America and which crossed the Atlantic, manned mostly by amateurs of Lake Superior experience(!), were still in one piece at the other end. She was definitely a single hander's dream and could look after herself like her illustrious name sake. Of course, a boat like that was not likely to win many races, which did not worry an old bomber pilot like myself, but her weight of eight and a half tons and two 5 foot galvanised steel bilge keels were not likely to allow her to perform aerobatics in a gale force wind either. Armed with that knowledge all that remained was our long awaited meeting with our dream boat.

We flew back to England and made our way to Plymouth without wasting a minute. Terry Erskine greeted us as arranged and took us straight from the railway station to the Sutton Marina. There she was! On the dull and damp February afternoon the sun shone in our hearts and we jumped for joy to the amusement of the few spectators. After that, having recovered our composure, we spent the evening with Terry soaking up his advice on the complicated process of commissioning our yacht for the 3000 mile voyage back to Cyprus. During the next seven days Hilda and I managed only one day at sea trying out every piece of Smoo-Cher's gear from the 21 hp Lister diesel to her Quartermaster self steering. The rest of our busy schedule consisted of purchasing stores and stowing everything neatly in the boat's spacious lockers, not forgetting extra fuel and water.

As daylight broke through another grey, overcast sky above the Sutton Marina on Friday, 22 February 1974, we said good-bye to Terry whose final words whispered in my ears were least encouraging.

'Remember what I said about marriage and sailing,' he said.

154

Grey morning in Plymouth – Setting off for Cyprus, 22 Feb 1974.

'Yes I know,' I whispered back looking at Hilda on the fore peak, 'two out of every five couples you sold the boats to, get divorced before reaching Gibraltar. You're not having me on, are you?'

'Don't worry Jack, it won't happen to you, but be careful and don't forget to write,' were his last words.

We hit the open lumpy sea with little wind to help us on the way while Smoo-Cher lost her dignity and tossed uncomfortably from side to side. Within minutes of passing the sombre, sea swept Eddyson lighthouse, the yacht's irregular movement sent my crew below. After refusing her plea to turn back and try again when weather improves. I sincerely hoped that throughout her totally incapacitating sea sickness which lasted 48 hours, that Terry Erskine's percentage prediction did not apply to us. Miraculously, on the third morning at sea my spouse emerged on deck and asked me what I wanted for my breakfast. For the rest of our long and demanding voyage she was never ill again.

We had now logged the first 300 miles, the moderate north easterly pushing us at a pleasing 5 knots across Biscay towards the

Spanish coast and the blue sky dispersing any remnants of the earlier disappointments. All that tranquillity, however, ended with the arrival of a delightfully playful school of dolphins which coincided with a gale warning on the radio and I immediately remembered the old sailor's adage:

'When the sea hog jumps, all hands to the pumps.'

Prepared as we were for bad weather this was a moment of truth. With a good deal of uncertainty at first we battled on in discomfort but in safety past Cape Finistere while Smoo-Cher looked after herself in heavy sea with a Force Eight wind on the quarter.

'I told you she can take it,' I exclaimed next day to my still frightened and unconvinced crew.

Needless to say, the Atlantic had more excitement in store for this prematurely overconfident skipper. On the afternoon, of 2nd March, we were 50 miles west of Lisbon making good progress southward, clear of the busy shipping lanes. I had selected this route remembering also the advice of my first flying instructor who believed that the hardest thing about flying was the ground and I applied this theory to sailing and the land, before even realising how important it would turn out to be on that day.

Up to 5 p.m. assisted by the Quartermaster, the stiff nor'wester gave us some of the best sailing to date but soon after this I decided to lower the main as sinister, fast-growing dark clouds appeared astern. The increasing wind whipped the wave tops and sent the spindrift sweeping across the surface. The barometer, which had fallen slowly during the past 48 hours, had now lost 5 milibars since lunch, confirming the approach of something nasty. In less than an hour the clearly defined scud roll cloud at the head of the approaching squall was upon us. The wind eased for a while, only to return with greater violence, stirring up the sea into a turmoil of spray and foam. A sudden torrential downpour cut visibility to a few hundred yards and all was dark, vicious and screaming. With hatches closed and the glistening white storm jib billowing in the gloom, Smoo-Cher sped down wind, first accelerating then slowing as the swell overtook us. At 7 p.m. the rain and clouds disappeared quickly, but the northerly gale continued, pushing the huge waves ahead of it. Stars flickered nervously as I stood in the hatch, with only my head and shoulders exposed to the elements, watching the sloop's perfect behaviour in the long Atlantic swell. I could not help comparing myself to a U-boat Commander at battle stations. The restraining grip of fear and uncertainty gave way again to the joys of overconfidence.

'What exhilarating sailing! Come and watch her run,' I shouted down below and even opened the hatch a little wider to allow the crew standing room next to me. Hilda did not share my enthusiasm. Just one glance at the white-crested mountains of water speeding past made her retire from the contest.

'This is madness,' she muttered. 'And how do you expect me to get the supper ready?' Her voice faded as she withdrew into the cabin below.

But the supper arrived as usual, be it only a mug of hot soup, a thick slice of brown bread and butter and a bar of chocolate. It tasted like heaven.

Reinforced, I resumed the watch, instructing my spouse to lie down and get as much rest as possible. I hoped that the weather would moderate and allow her an easier time later. As it was, the opposite happened and within two hours the nor'wester reached Storm Force. The fierce whistling and howling began to unnerve me. Holding on to the coamings I felt my hands shake. The pressure on the boat was enormous. She raced on under the storm jib only, touching nine knots but, as her designers predicted, the Golden Hind had mercifully no tendency to broach. This was just as well, because the forces involved made any alteration of her heading quite impossible. Crouched down in the cockpit, I held on now to the lashed down tiller seeking protection from the biting wind and spray. Ragged patches of clouds streaked past the half moon, as I watched our 32 foot high mast being dwarfed by the running waves and awaited disaster with the approach of each curly white monster.

Soon after 2 a.m. the wind eased to an estimated Force 8. I glanced at the log. It read 800 miles. This, most encouraging discovery, meant that we had travelled 51 miles in the last 6 hours, mostly in the right direction. At about the same time, my brave crew emerged and ordered me to bed.

But the ordeal was not over yet. Two hours later I hurried back to the cockpit, rubbing my half shut eyes in search of the reported light.

The rude awakening took place within seconds. A huge shadow outlined by two mast lights and the starboard green emerged out of the massive swell no more than two cables away on our port quarter. The big tanker, heading south was obviously empty and tossed grotesquely in the rough sea ignoring our insignificant presence. Disregarding my torch signals, she continued ahead on the collision course, plunging out of sight and reappearing larger than ever. At last, as I prepared to fire a pyro across her bridge, she began to turn slowly away and the uneven confrontation was over. For a while we could see her crew on the bridge peering into the darkness towards us and probably disbelieving their eyes.

How on earth Hilda made coffee that night, I do not know, but we needed it badly. We sipped the hot liquid and in the darkness watched the lights of several other vessels to port and starboard. It was apparent that we had entered the southbound traffic zone around Cape St Vincent. It also meant that the wind and tide had made our yacht drift at least 20 miles further east than our intended track. Later that morning, I altered course for the Gibraltar Straits. The sight of the forbidding, rocky Portuguese coast pounded by the angry Atlantic swell, which continued long after the storm abated, gave me the shivers at the thought what would have happened if we had been closer to it the night before. Wisely, I did not share these deliberations with Hilda who, after a short prayer, was busy stowing away the distress rockets and plastic bags with food and drinks she had prepared for the liferaft. I felt immensely sorry for her and could only say: 'It's all over, Darling, we're safe . . . tomorrow we're in the Mediterranean.'

After motoring for the next 28 hours in a flat calm, we arrived in Gibraltar practically out of fuel and retired to the nearest hotel completely exhausted.

It is amazing what a hot bath and a 12 hour sleep do for the sailor. Immediately after breakfast I was on my way, still swaying from side to side on terra firma, to organise refuelling and the replacements for the phosphorous bronze shackle and the eye in the clew of the storm jib which should have lasted for ever. There was also another outstanding business I had to attend to. Sending postcards from Gibraltar to announce our arrival was no problem as far as the United Kingdom was concerned but I was anxious to let my Station

Commander in Cyprus know about my progress. He had authorised my six weeks leave and I felt obliged not to cause him a nervous breakdown. I left Hilda on board, who fortunately did not seek the lawyers or any society preventing cruelty to wives, and headed for the Royal Air Force station situated on the north side of the Rock. I hurried past the customs post and through an estate of grey, featureless blocks of flats, gaudily displaying the clashing colours of window curtains and fluttering white washing. Towering above it all, the vertical, bare slopes of the mighty fortress seemed to contemplate the price of progress.

I was shown into the office of Air Commodore Sutton, who commanded Royal Air Force Gibraltar, by a smart female personal assistant. It did not take me long to ascertain that I was introduced to a man keenly interested in the sea and sailing.

'How extraordinary!' he exclaimed. 'You must have gone through the same storm which almost wrecked the new P&O ferry Eagle. She was on her way back from Tangier when shifting cargo smashed a large hole in her side. We had two Shackletons looking for her after the Mayday call.'

'What happened to her in the end?' I asked excitedly.

'Oh, she managed to make Lisbon where she will stay for quite some time for repairs.' He got up from behind the desk shook my hand. 'I would very much like to see your boat and meet your brave wife,' he added.

The signal to Cyprus was duly dispatched and in the afternoon we greeted the Air Commodore aboard Smoo-Cher. We learned that the strong easterly wind which was now rocking all the boats in the marina is known locally as the Levanter. 'This devil usually blows for three days or so but has been known to last three weeks,' our guest explained before offering us any assistance we may need and even an invitation to the Officers Mess. I felt though that this was too early to start the return to civilised existence and declined the offer hoping down deep that his depressing wind prognosis would not materialise.

Back in the hotel for the final clean up Hilda and I counted the dark bruises on our bodies and painful cracks on our fingers wrongly expecting the end of further suffering.

It is said that all comes to those who wait. In my case it all happened to the one who could not wait. With less than 4 weeks of my leave left and 2000 miles to go we set off from Gibraltar on 9th March unable to linger in expectation of fair winds. Despite the Admiralty Pilot's prediction of 70 to 90 per cent westerly winds at this time of the year, our Smoo-Cher encountered head winds for almost the whole length of the Mediterranean. It caused us unscheduled stops at Trapani in Sicily, in Malta and the Greek island of Kithira which on an unlimited time schedule could have been a dream come true. As it was, three days of the swirling, dusty, gale force Sirocco before we had even reached Sicily made me write 'TOTAL FRUSTRATION' across the full page of boat's log book before Hilda and I dropped on the cabin floor completely out of steam. The hove-to yacht looked after herself for 24 hours and drifted 30 miles westwards in the open sea. Determined to make up for the lost time I left Valetta in a Force 6 north easterly after replenishing our dwindling supplies, leaving occupiers of the luxury yachts there with mouths wide open.

Soon after, another newcomer registered its name in my log book. It was what the Arabs call 'Ghibli'. This gale, even dirtier than the Sirocco, met us head on 50 miles west of Crete. The sand lifted from the desert south of Tobruk in Libya obliterated blue skies and, in the middle of the day, the Mediterranean sun acquired the brightness of a watery moon. The ever increasing worry about the condition of my long suffering wife prompted me in the end to alter course for Iraklion in Crete, the nearest airport from which she could return to Cyprus via Athens. However, before my plan could materialise, the fickle wind veered south and finally, a westerly gale enabled us to reach Cyprus, 400 miles ahead, only 5 days behind our original schedule.

On a warm but still windy afternoon, on 10th April, we entered Larnaca Marina and moored in one of the many empty berths. The relief of being able to discard our weatherproofs after all this time was apparent. Hilda threw her sailing suit the full length of the cabin floor in an act of defiance and finality.

'That's that for me!' she shouted, ' . . . and I hope not to wear you ever again!'

160

Back home in Nicosia our bathroom scales revealed the true physical strain of our endeavour. I now weighed 145 pounds, nearly 30 pounds lighter and Hilda, who at the end of the voyage had acquired a new name of Jynxy and lost a stone and a half, something she could never had achieved by dieting. After just seven weeks we were able to display the finest assortment of ribs outside of Belsen. Not that the thought worried us as we laid down in our soft-sprung double bed, and felt it float up and down and away into a dreamland.

CHAPTER 10

Into The Fire Again

Amidst the soaring temperatures of the following May and June, I was busy at work compensating everyone for my extended absence. An occasional visit to see Smoo-Cher in Larnaca brightened my days. It was very fortunate that she had arrived in such good shape and required practically no attention at all. Hilda, now a confirmed sceptic about the life at sea, managed, nevertheless, to raise enough enthusiasm to look proudly after Smoo-Cher. I doubt if there was a smarter or cleaner yacht in the whole of the marina. The self-designed, home made cotton awnings kept the sun off her forehatch, mainsail and the cockpit where timbers shone like new after a generous application of teak oil. I found as much pleasure in the harbour chores as in a rare weekend at sea. The local sea breezes made Larnaca Bay anything but the blue lagoon depicted on postcards, and I often reefed unashamedly as winds in excess of 20 miles-per-hour rushed inland to fill the vacuum created by the searing heat of the midday sun. Good and exciting sailing I called it, although not all of my guests agreed. Back in the marina the unusual sight then in Cyprus of an ocean going sloop brought many admiring visitors, and I must confess we enjoyed their attention.

Larnaca, a sleepy provincial town in the process of being modernised, offered a mixture of characteristic Cypriot hospitality from a divided population of Greek and Turkish origin. Overlooking the new harbour with its most accommodating, up-to-date marina was a modern block of flats and a hotel. They stood in vivid contrast to the remainder of a pleasantly neglected forefront, where beneath the swaying palms, a variety of colourfully illuminated stalls and

163

tavernas tempted the evening passers-by with an aroma of charcoal cooked kebabs. There at the end of each visit, we counted our blessings over a meal and a glass of wine, watching the constant drift of cars and pedestrians or just admiring the light reflections in the still water.

By the time July arrived we had visited most of the coves and beaches on the south coast. On occasions when Smoo-Cher was resting I managed to give Jynxy a break from sailing by visiting our old hide-outs in Kyrenia. The poor lass continued to attract a stiff breeze within minutes of boarding the yacht, something she was beginning to dislike thoroughly about Larnaca Bay. Mainly for that reason I started to look forward to September and my long awaited leave, planning a leisurly cruise to the north coast of Cyprus where one can spend days at anchor in sheltered coves without a breath of wind.

Cyprus, as always, was full of rumours and political speculations, but ominously, for the first time, the rift between Athens and President Makarios was openly trumpeted by the local media. Nevertheless, the 6.00 a.m. bombshell of Friday, 15 July, took everyone by surprise. Hilda and I were awakened by sporadic shooting followed by the clatter of tanks along the airport road only 20 yards from our bedroom window. We did not know then that after a bloody battle at the airport terminal further down the road, the loyal government police force had been overcome and the way was already cleared for the Greek Army to move against the presidential palace. We watched their progress with great foreboding and a feeling of sadness for Cyprus and its people. Soon the sound of heavy guns and mortars echoed across the stricken city and thick black smoke billowed over the palace. In the afternoon Cyprus radio prematurely announced that Makarios was dead and the union with Greece was accomplished.

Throughout the coup the British contingent at Nicosia was confined to camp, and as ordered, maintained a 'low profile' and the traditional native phlegm to boot. Being unarmed and politically neutralised we could do little else, anyway. National Guard units supported by the Greek Army took over all communications at the airport, flying ceased and the air traffic systems came to a grinding halt. But we continued to man our posts confronted by machine guns held nervously by the young revolutionaries at each entrance, while pregnant silence prevailed. On the third day after the coup my phone did ring. It was one of the cranking variety called 'field telephone' which must have been salvaged from the Verdun trenches and was installed years ago as a back-up to not as reliable modern systems. Surprised to hear it for the first time, I managed to pick it up slowly, aware of undivided attention of every eyeball in the control room. The line was weak and intermittent.

'Who's that?' a faint voice seemed to come from another planet.

'RAF controller Nicosia.'

'Who?'

'RAF controller Nicosia,' I repeated a little louder.

'Oh, at last! Operations . . . trying to get you . . . how long before your chaps . . . move the tanks off the runway . . . Akrotiri is short of diversions . . .' Here the line expired for good, and after a few pointless 'hallos' I casually replaced the receiver. My disappointed audience returned to a more relaxed posture. 'Just as well,' I said to myself. Apart from being rude there was no answer to this question, and it dawned on me that if anyone on our side actually knew what was going on he would not part with the secret. On the same day we learned from a helicopter pilot of 84 Squadron that they had rescued Makarios from a hide out in Paphos although the pilot himself was wounded by the ground fire. So much for Nato unity!

No one believed the Turks either. Five days after the coup, despite their ultimatum threatening an imminent military intervention, things began to return to normal and we were allowed free travel during the hours of daylight. It goes without saying that our first destination was Larnaca. We listened on the car radio to the grim news of the Turkish invasion fleet assembling to the north and nervously wondered if Smoo-Cher had survived unscathed during the reported fighting between Greeks and Turks in Larnaca. I drove slowly through the almost deserted streets. Except for the well guarded group of Turks huddled together in a school courtyard and some nasty looking bullet holes in and around the mosque, the town showed no visible signs of its recent upheaval. To our relief everything aboard Smoo-Cher was intact. Our arrival in the marina

165

brought out a few of our local friends, including Marios and Andreas, who greeted us warmly, but this time the instant Cypriot smiles were missing and their carefree attitude gone. After some trivial exchanges, Andreas, an elderly marine official, came close to me and whispered in my ear: 'Why didn't you British intervene? This should never have happened.'

I shrugged my shoulders trying to prove my ignorance but sensing a search for a scapegoat anywhere but home replied: 'My friend, lucky for me I am not a politician but it seems to me that the British have not enough practice in bringing their governments down by force and simply don't know what to do about it.'

As our visitors departed we wished them any luck going while we lingered on board well into the afternoon, reluctant to leave our treasured possession again, yet unable to alter the course of events. Finally, our empty stomachs prompted us to return to Nicosia.

At 5.00 p.m. the 'Dust Bowl' was still red hot, and within the concrete of Nicosia we felt doubly uncomfortable. In Metaxas Square, normally teeming with Friday evening customers, most of the shops were closed and the pavements empty. Those who were hoping for business as usual were now hurriedly putting the shutters down and driving off at speed. Despite an air of indifference on the part of the local disc jockey, whose electronic paraphernalia boomed out last year's hits, there hung a depressing atmosphere of tense expectation over the whole city. Hungry and thirsty, we returned home.

The shock of seeing Greeks fighting Greeks a week ago paled in comparison with the hell that broke loose at dawn on Saturday. Turkish fighter bombers struck hard and true. The Greek Army camp across the airport road disintegrated under the aerial bombardment that sprayed our roofs with shrapnel and loose rock. The proximity of the earth-splitting explosions combined with the heavy machine gun fire of the surrounding defenders made me leap out of bed, completely awake, yet disorientated. From under the sheets Hilda's hysterical cries could be heard above the din.

'Good God, what's happening? Jack, Jack, where are you!? Come back . . . we're going to die, oh, God!'

The first attack lasted about ten minutes. With the departure of the screaming jets an equally noticeable silence took over. I peered carefully through the shutters, but there was nothing to see except clouds of smoke and dust.

'Come on Jynxy.' I said turning to my shaking spouse, 'we've got to get organised. These prefab walls couldn't stop a cream cake.'

I put my arms around her and guided her gently towards the lounge and the only stone wall of our house. The second attack came just then, suddenly and with a deafening ferocity. I flung myself on the floor taking Hilda with me. Now, I was shaking and had to use all my will power to regain my wits. More bombs were falling and again we could hear the rattle of thrown up debris on the roof tiles. It was clear that any sizeable bomb or shell fragment falling on top of the house would not be prevented from coming right through the ceiling. I scanned the room for protection. Yes, that will do! Our solid oak dining room table. We pushed it against the stone wall. Outside there was another break in the air raid. I dashed back through the bedrooms and brought mattresses, pillows and blankets. Soon we had a comfortable shelter stacked with remaining furniture and lined on all sides with bedding. Jynxy, who was fast recovering from the initial panic, settled in the den instructing me to join her at the first sound of fire. In between the outbursts of sporadic shooting I managed to make toast and coffee and prepared two flasks of iced squash for later. The sudden arrival of our military police van on the married patch ordering everyone to stay put added the only humorous interlude to our existence. 'And don't listen to rumours,' concluded the announcer.

For the rest of the day air attacks continued at regular intervals of about half an hour, with the addition of low level strafing by the Turkish F100s. I had heard of the dreaded Vulcan cannon before but had never considered the possibility of being at its mercy. The destructive effect of 6000 shells per minute gave little chance of survival in the vicinity of any target let alone from the terrorising, grinding sound of each burst which vibrated for miles around making us wish we could burrow a few hundred feet below the ground. Bitterly I began to unfold my erratic progress since my escape from Warsaw in 1939.

' . . . I should have known from the start . . . at seventeen bombed

167

out of my own home, a year later blasted out of France . . . shot at by ack ack and night fighters . . . chased by the doodle bugs in London and even shot at in "peacetime" Malaya . . . my last bloody tour couldn't be any different . . . you weren't careful enough when you married me, Jynxy.'

In the distance, defending ack ack began to rumble with an increasing intensity. 'Get back this instant!' Hilda yelled, ignoring my morbid comment and withdrawing deeper into the shelter. As I scrambled in beside her a violent explosion shook the bungalow to its foundations. We heard a tinkling crash as the hall light hit the floor. Loose debris and shrapnel raked the roof tiles and our nostrils filled with a musty smell of loose plaster and flaking wallpaint. Hilda grabbed me with both hands. I could feel her body tremble all over.

'Hell, that was close,' I heard myself speak with relief, but seeing an expression of horror in front of me, my morale sagged to a new depth. I held her tightly. 'There, there, darling, after all it did miss us . . .'

With the departure of the raiders all shooting died down suddenly and an eerie silence clamped down upon us once again. The electric fan left on the floor continued to hum ineffectively sending searing hot air against our freely perspiring bodies. I wiped the running sweat off my eyes and mustered what bravado I had left.

'Come on, Jynxy, if we have to die let's do it in comfort. We're as sticky as hell, it's time for a shower.'

A few minutes later she observed my return. I must have looked temptingly fresh with a glass of brandy sour in my hand. Without a word Hilda picked herself up, slung her dressing gown across her shoulders, and ran for the bathroom.

It was now mid-afternoon and my stomach was playing a prelude to starvation. I went into the kitchen in search of a meal. Despite one short interruption by an attacking aircraft and a panicky visit from Patrick next door, who produced a spade cut in half on his patio by shrapnel, I managed to create a meal of two succulent grilled steaks with trimmings and proudly announced that dinner was ready. To my great disappointment, Hilda did not share my enthusiasm. Still looking pale and shaken she could not face a morsel of food. However, she watched me with some amazement, as I worked through the double course, and finally joined me for coffee.

Fortunately for them, most of the young children in our neighbourhood had left the day before for England with their parents, at the start of school holidays. When evening came and the bombing stopped, we found out that except for Patrick, the weatherman, and his family all remaining inhabitants of our street had moved to safety into the stone built houses further away from the Greek Army camp. Alas, the latter has disappeared into history and we felt secure in our shelter. We decided to stay put.

During the night the Greek Army brought up their heavy artillery to the rear of our quarter and began to pound the Turkish held Kyrenia Mountains. Soon the thickly wooded slopes were set ablaze. The booming, nerve racking discharges offered no chance of rest or sleep , and we watched the grim, pulsating red glow of the distant fires, which by midnight, radiated like a volcanic erruption. Our usual Cyprus 'crack of dawn' chorus of sparrows did not materialise but with daylight the sinister birds of war returned. Predictably, their efforts were concentrated on enemy gun positions behind us. Once again the air filled with thunderous jets, screeching Vulcan cannon and exploding bombs. Their targets were a few hundred yards away from our house, and thankfully for us, their aim was accurate. At 7:00 a.m. still under the table, we listened intently to the Forces broadcast. Instead of the news we heard a repeated warning to all British nationals to stand by for an important announcement. Jynxy regained some confidence. 'At last,' she exclaimed, 'someone has realised there is a war on.' Nonetheless, for three hours we had to listen to the latest string of activities within the Sovereign Base Areas on the island, such as bingo and flower arranging classes, interspersed by musical requests. Rather than throw the radio across the room I swore at it crudely between each record. Outside one could hear the steady staccato of machine guns and explosions that sounded like mortar fire or hand grenades. 'That's a ground attack!' My thoughts came out loudly, yet disbelievingly. Hilda closed her eyes as if in prayer and seemed to shrink even further within herself. A sudden screech of tyres turned our attention to the front of the house. A loudhailer boomed out across the street: 'We are being evacuated . . . pack a bag and be ready to move in five minutes . . .

further instructions will follow ... I say again ...' Before the message could be repeated, Hilda and I were running in all directions in search of essentials and valuables. Every glance around the bungalow cut deeply into our hearts, as an imminent loss of togetherness loomed nearer with each passing minute. I carried two suitcases and put them on the back seat of our car. Someone came running by. 'Convoy is assembling by the Medical Centre!' I heard him shout. We drove away without looking back.

The only consolation to our numbed minds came soon after, when we joined the rest of our battered neighbourhood. What the hell, after all we were all in the same stew and the same fate awaited us. Tension soon eased. Under a proud, although limp, Union Jack, the large convoy of service and private vehicles moved slowly away into the heat haze ahead. Despite the sporadic, piercing bangs of mortar shells on both sides along the road to the centre of Nicosia, our convoy suffered no casualties and we saw no panic or disorder among the families. Ahead of the mighty war machine pushing down from the north, the city itself showed only few scars. There was no sign of fighting here, but a typically sad trek of refugees, burdened under their possessions, grew in numbers until by the Hilton hotel, the roads were packed with escaping humanity using all means of transport from village buses to bicycles. Also there, a large British force of armour waited grimly in the side streets. We were delighted to see them and later watched the heavy armoured cars take up their escort stations within our evergrowing convoy. During the afternoon of the same scorching day, we made a slow, uneventful journey of the remaining twenty miles to the south coast. The wide eyed residents of the British Sovereign Base at Dhekelia saw us enter their garrison looking cheerless and weary although, deep inside, very much relieved.

Some things one can never get used to. As the novelty of 'near miss' and 'close shave' stories lost its attraction, my forgotten feeling of an evacuee's resignation and depression returned with a vengeance. Within hours we became part of Dhekelia's swarming population of escaping Greek Cypriots, tourists of every nationality and even diplomatic staffs, all caught up in the crossfire of war. The pressure was on.

170

For twelve days, besides looking after ourselves, we helped the overworked garrison in the processing and evacuation of the refugees. Most of them were in possession of British passports and were flown out to the United Kingdom. After that, our group was moved 50 miles west to the top of the Troodos mountains, where we acquired the title of Nicosia Nomads. We occupied winter chalets and tents of this skiing resort in the delightful warmth of mid-summer, breathing in the crystal clear air at six thousand feet above sea level. Still, the persistent concern about our future and the fate of Smoo-Cher hung over Jynxy and myself, spoiling an otherwise idyllic relaxation after the recent, shattering events. In the meantime, United Nations troops, mainly British, prevented the Turks from occupying the International Airport, and elsewhere the tense military situation became static. Well, so it seemed.

At dawn on the second day of the final Turkish offensive, which cut Cyprus in two, a sharp knock on the door got me out of bed. We were to assemble once again in a convoy; our destination this time, Akrotiri. There followed the usual few minutes of panic, gathering of belongings, a fruitless inquiry, 'what is it all about,' a touch of unwanted breakfast, and we were snaking down a steep and narrow road towards another British base. Before anyone could recover from the shock news, we were repacking our two suitcases in front of the Akrotiri transit mess. My Jynxy, with the rest of the Nicosia families was being sent back to England. I held her tight and kissed her tearful face. I saw her turn towards me as, already filled with sadness and despair she reluctantly boarded the coach . . . The suddenness and finality of her departure stunned me to the core. Heavy hearted, I contemplated my cruel fate. My dear and devoted pal gone, carefully and bravely executed plans for retirement were now in ruins. What of Smoo-Cher's fate? Was she still in Larnaca . . . and if so, was she still in one piece? What now of the homely little treasures and all that happiness in Nicosia?

Predictably I felt sorry for myself. After a lifetime of hard battles and demanding, even though self inflicted, ambitions I tasted the bitterness of what seemed a conclusive defeat. Nothing could be done now and there was nothing left . . . at least on that one sad day in Akrotiri, 15th August 1974.

Four days later I was still in the madhouse of the vastly overcrowded Akrotiri. Since Mother Nature and the Royal Air Force would not allow me to stagnate, I was no longer depressed although still sore. My Nicosia colleagues and I were busy once again assisting in the evacuation of thousands of mainly Service or Service employed civilian families. Unhappily, we witnessed yet another bastion of a once-mighty Empire crumble in front of us. During those few days the Turkish military steamroller crushed all remaining resistance in its path. Famagusta fell, and the slow but persistent advance towards Larnaca continued. Many brave people died for one cause or another and there seemed no respite for the tormented island.

Now I had to do something about Smoo-Cher and put my plans in front of the Commanding Officer. There was a complete ban on travel by land. My idea was to hitch a lift on one of the regular helicopter flights between Akrotiri and Dhekelia and be off-loaded on the way, near the Larnaca marina. From there I could sail Smoo-Cher back to the Akrotiri Mole and berth her within the safety of the Sovereign Base Area. My friend Ron Dench gamely offered to assist and to crew. Gratefully I heard a day later that HQ Operations approved the scheme. Some kind soul even helped to organise an Army staff car to take us as near to the marina as possible, when it was decided that landing a helicopter amidst the chaos of retreating population was too dangerous.

Ron and I arrived on the outskirts of Larnaca on 20th August at 5:00 p.m. and thanked the driver and escort for the lift. Gingerly we made our way through packed streets towards the Customs House. The remains of regular and partly uniformed soldiery were rubbing shoulders with refugees and what was left of Larnaca's inhabitants. One or two grocer shops and some coffee houses, which were still open, were swamped with business, spilling their customers across the already overcrowded pavements. The sound of human voices was unnaturally subdued, many a man glancing over his shoulders in nervous anticipation. The Turks were only six miles away and who could tell if they would stop. Come to that, Ron and I felt the same twitch. The electric atmosphere around us caused us to increase our pace as we bustled and squeezed through. At last we reached the sea front. Here we found the Customs House shut and all port offices closed. In contrast to the scene in town, we looked now through an open unguarded gate at the almost deserted marina. There was only one boat in sight and that was Smoo-Cher. My heart skipped a beat at the first sight of her. She sat alone, nice and snug, with a kind of dignity that calm waters give to a boat. I ran all the way past the endless deserted berths. It took only one glance at her deck to realise that she was unmarked, and all the gear, including the expensive life-raft, untouched. I was delighted and full of admiration for this unbelievable show of honesty in the most tempting, panic stricken situation.

Our instant aim was a quick getaway. I prayed that the Lister would live up to its reputation after being static for weeks. There was plenty of fuel on board and in the still air of the evening it was just as well. I unlocked the hatch and found again everything intact. In minutes we stowed away the sail and cockpit covers, slackened off the moorings, and were ready to go. Just then Ron pointed towards two uniformed men approaching from the far end of the pier. 'Here comes trouble,' he mumbled. Before we could decide what to do next the loud footsteps on the timber planking were upon us. I heard a familiar voice. 'Hello Jack, are you leaving us also?'

It was Marios. Dressed in the uniform of a Lieutenant of the National Guard and armed with a pistol, he looked strangely solemn. I invited him on board and suggested a Scotch for the sake of old times. I knew he liked it and I poured out a fair measure. Afterwards it was natural to sit in the cockpit, for nothing is done in Cyprus without a chair and a drink to start with. Our departure had to wait. One or two sips of the Celtic mountain dew were sufficient to relax a somewhat tense atmosphere and tongues loosened a great deal. Marios spent the initial days of the invasion defending Kyrenia. He did not enlarge on many details but it was obvious from what he said that the battle was bitter and bloody. He withdrew with his unit to Larnaca and was put in charge of the harbour.

'Since then,' Marios continued, 'we have had many inquiries about your whereabouts, Jack. One Lebanese armed with a suitcase full of American dollars was desperate to buy your boat and is still waiting somewhere nearby.'

'Nothing doing,' I retorted strongly, 'but thank you, Marios, for looking after my ship in my absence. You're a pal!'

The effect of whisky and my sincerity had a depressing effect on my highly emotional Cypriot friend, and I was confronted by two fiery dark eyes openly shedding tears of defiance.

'Never mind the past! I promise you that next year I will treat you personally in Kyrenia . . . even if we have to die a hundred times we shall get them out, we will, you'll see . . .

He downed the remains of his glass, quickly wiped his face, shook my hand and jumped ashore.

'By the way where are you going from here?'

'Akrotiri Mole.'

'Bon voyage, Jack.'

'Thank you again, Marios. May happiness return to your country soon and all your wishes come true.'

We could still hear the heavy Army boots on the pier when I pressed the starter. The healthy sound of an accelerating diesel filled the air and echoed across the water.

'Good old Lister!' I shouted to smiling Ron up forward. 'Cast off!'

Smoo-Cher sneaked out of Larnaca in almost total darkness. We motored all night, rounding Cape Kiti at a respectable distance and keeping well off shore for the rest of the journey. As the stars faded in the east, we entered Akrotiri Mole. That long lost feeling of confidence and achievement began to creep back under my skin.

A few weeks later I returned to Nicosia with the rest of the 'Nomads' to man the British retained site and to re-establish communications for the United Nations helicopters of 84 Squadron. From the Air Traffic building I watched the sign on the roof of the bullet ridden terminal building, once proudly lit up day and night, leaning at a peculiar angle and showing gaps where four large letters were missing in the words: NIC SIA INTERNAT O AL AI PORT. In the distance, on the runway laid the shattered remains of an airliner, adding to the ghostly appearance of the scene around me. I found our married quarter still there, but I was glad that Hilda was not there to see it after it had been ransacked by troops coming and going in our absence, although it must be said that in our bungalow only food and some bedding was missing, obvious essentials in any soldier's field situation.

When the first heavy autumn rains descended on Cyprus I was wearing the blue beret of the United Nations knowing that this was a start of a nine month unaccompanied tour. My Jynxy settled down in a Brize Norton married quarter on her own hoping that it would be a most convenient place for my subsequent arrival. As it happened, the only time I managed to get on an aeroplane during that time on a week's leave, it took me to Gatwick 120 miles away!

The year of 1975 turned out to be a decision time. With only fifteen months left to my retirement Hilda and I decided to stick to our original plan to live in Cyprus for at least a few years and see how things develop. I was sick and tired of running away into even worse circumstances then I had experienced previously, our pride and joy was safely moored on the British Base and we could not forget the pleasures of blue water and sunshine. And so I applied for an extension of my tour until the last day of my service. This paid dividends even though I had to move twice between Nicosia and Akrotiri filling the posts of a departing Senior Air Traffic Controller and then an Operations Officer who left on compassionate grounds. During those temporary appointments I was not entitled to any official accompanied accommodation but it was not difficult to find a home on the island in the days when nearly half of the Cyprus population had left for Greece, the United Kingdom and even as far away as Australia. I managed to bring Hilda back on an indulgence flight from Brize Norton and after only few days aboard Smoo-Cher she was able to move into a modern house in the village of Erimi, 8 miles from Akrotiri. I was delighted! It also signalled a beginning of our most rewarding association with the completely unspoiled life of the village people who were confronted by the very first British residents. Hilda's modern appearance and blond hair became an object of immense interest to all the Erimi women and invitations to coffee poured out from almost every house each time she stepped out of our door. Whenever I arrived after work there was also the serious problem of having to refuse the menfolk a pleasure of sharing with me a bottle of local brew, some 90 per cent proof. We must have attended every wedding and engagement party during the first year

175

of our stay there but we felt greatly relieved after that when the novelty of our appearance gradually faded and allowed us a little rest from the constant feeding, and Greek dancing.

By the time my retirement materialised on Christmas Eve 1976 we were quite prepared for the life in this new environment and only the question of our own permanent home which Jynxy had pined for for so many years, remained unanswered. Two years later, thanks to the help from the local people, we acquired a piece of a recently abandoned orchard overlooking the Kouris river valley, in sight of the sea, and began the construction of our house. I used my limited and nearly forgotten skills of a budding architect and had my design approved by the district office while the village masons and labourers, under our strict supervision, toiled with sand, cement, bricks and hundreds of marble tiles to make another dream come true.

When we finally moved in and restored the gardens with variety of citrus trees and masses of flowers I remember sitting on the patio facing the setting sun with a glass of cold beer in my hand and teasing my dear Jynxy with the usual masculine conceit.

'There, my Love, I told you I will give you a garden of Eden one day, and here it is.' She looked at me without a hint of gratitude and replied: 'How can it be? There is not a single apple tree in it.'

We laughed.

CHAPTER I I

Return Of The Warrior

When Aunt Zofia died in 1989 1 thought that she was my last close relative in Poland who had parted company with this world. A strange, but hitherto unknown to me, branch of our family tree proved me wrong after I received a letter in Cyprus from Malgosia. She took care of my auntie until her death and later helped to wrap up all the affairs connected with her departure. She was in fact the long forgotten niece of my mother and Aunt Zofia and therefore, my first cousin. Malgosia's mother, born 20 years after her sisters, probably an after-thought on part of my maternal grandad, produced a daughter well after the war when I was already in my thirties. This pleasant discovery of a so much younger close relative, started months of correspondence and coincided with the sudden and unexpected disintegration of the Soviet Union and the return of independence to Poland. Back here in Cyprus I could not help but hope to see for myself what was left of my country after half a century of occupation and indoctrination and, of course, to meet my newly discovered cousin.

Our annual Christmas visit to our son, now the headmaster of a junior school in Durham, was in the offing and I decided to combine this with a Polish adventure by flying to London via Warsaw. To make it more attractive for Jynxy I asked Malgosia to book for us a hotel room for a week which included 13th December, our golden wedding anniversary that year.

The Polish Air Lines Ilyushin landed on the frozen runway of Mokotow Airport 10 hours late, after delays which occurred en route to Larnaca, and we disembarked into the prefabricated buildings of the old Warsaw terminal teeming with travellers, armed police and local staff. It took another two hours to clear a rather primitive customs and immigration desk and we were convinced that Malgosia would not be there to greet us as arranged. But we were wrong. As soon as we entered the arrival lounge a smartly dressed, attractive female rushed towards us and fell into my arms.

'My dear, dear Jacek . . . I thought I would never meet you in this world!'

A few tears and hugs later she turned to Hilda and squeezed her tightly. This time she spoke excitedly in English. 'I recognised you both immediately from the photographs your mother left behind. Come, come, you must be worn out, I have a taxi waiting.'

The Hotel Metropole was one of the two original buildings still standing in the centre of the city. The six storeys of this pre-war 5 star remnant were, nevertheless, dwarfed by a monstrosity of concrete which, I learned later, was erected by the Russians as a 'gift' to Polish people and named, in the true character of the Soviet rulers, 'Palace of Culture'. Beneath this skyscraper hundreds of small traders filled the huge open area with simply constructed stalls, peddling everything from home made bread rolls to second hand electrical fittings. Ironically, I was witnessing the first signs of human resilience and ingenuity at the end of a complete ban on private enterprise by the State.

We entered the portals of our hotel assisted by uniformed porters and while unpacking in our suite we settled to a session of questions and answers which only ended after the arrangements for the following day were made between the three of us. The thick walls, double glazed heavy windows and heavy curtains cut out all the external sounds as Hilda and I dropped off into an uninterrupted and well deserved sleep. Even after eight hours it was not easy to climb out of the enclosing warmth of the feather filled bedding. I drew the curtains and looked outside.

'Get up Jynxy and have a look at this,' I enthused like a little boy at the sight of Father Christmas, 'it is snowing!'

In the distance, like a granite mountain, the outline of the 'Palace' was just visible through the falling snowflakes but down below the undeterred but heavily wrapped up stall holders were already getting ready for business. Malgosia, who stayed with her friend during this visit to Warsaw, arrived soon after our breakfast and I reminded myself that winter here brings no fear to the hearts of the inhabitants.

As we walked outside, determined to see as much as possible of the largely reconstructed capital, and in my case, enter the long awaited memory lane, I had to satisfy my curiosity around every corner of the drastically changed scene.

'Yes, I remember it now. Isn't this where the Central Station was?' I asked. Malgosia nodded. 'Yes, the whole of the city centre here was torn out by the German bombing and later in 1944 even the ruins were set alight.'

'How on earth did mother survive all this? There were several platforms here . . . Rafal and I said goodbye to her in this very place.'

'Didn't you live somewhere on the south side of the town?'

'Yes, I remember the address. It was Olesinska No 5, a modern block of 4 flats. I must see what happened to it, also my old school is not so far from there.'

We boarded the Warsaw tram which seemed like something recalled to service from 50 years ago. Twenty minutes later the conductor pointed us to one of the side streets some 100 meters from the tram stop. 'That's Olesinska over there.' I felt my knees giving way and a strange tightning inside my belly.

The scene at first did not look familiar. A tightly packed, uniformly built, grey residential estate stretched on both sides of the main Mokotow thoroughfare as far as I could see. Only one house was different, tucked away in the side street. The three of us walked gingerly towards it. There was no doubt about it, this was the house I was brought up in 54 years ago! No 5 was still pinned to the main entrance, now in a pitiful state of neglect, paint and varnish peeling off and bits of plaster on the steps. I walked up to the first floor on a wide staircase flanked by the disintegrating bannisters and faced the bolted, bare wood door. Is this really the place I used to walk in and out of as a boy feeling the warmth of family around me? I felt tears running down my cheeks, turned away from the door and unable to control my emotions, walked down the stairs again hastily wiping my face dry.

'Guess what we found,' greeted Hilda in a sombre mood.

A few metres from the main entrance a large display of red and white fresh cut flowers filled part of the remaining front wall which I thought at first was just an enterprising florist business. Sadly, a memorial plaque in the centre of the decoration revealed another act of man's inhumanity to man. Loosely translated it read:

'Against this wall 26 Polish patriots who fought for our country's freedom in 1944 were shot by the Gestapo. Let us not forget them.'

An elderly passer-by, seeing us staring at the memorial, tried to be helpful.

'This was a Gestapo headquarters, you know. During the uprising in 1944 the Germans wiped out more people here in Warsaw than the bomb did in Hiroshima. There weren't many houses left when the Russians arrived, only crosses.'

I walked away without saying a word but my long lasting, yet secret twinges of guilt over my part in destruction of the German cities vanished for ever that morning. Later, I found an empty site where my Lyceum stood amongst greenery and sport fields of a parkland.

After that depressing session things had to improve, and they did. We alighted from the tram two stops before our destination and walked the rest of the way past several more permanent shops to the great satisfaction of my companions. I was surprised how quickly they took to each other, chatting freely and sharing everyday feminine interests even though Malgosia's English was far from perfect. Seeing the abundance of food displayed by the grocers and particularly the huge meat joints in most butcher shops I could not help but reminisce again.

'Good God, what a transformation,' I said loudly. 'I remember Aunt Zofia queueing in Luban at six in the morning for a loaf of bread!'

Malgosia threw her pretty head back in an angry posture. 'So now we know where all the food went in the last 50 years. To Russia, of course, and furthermore,' she continued hardly taking a breath, 'our Army had to double the frontier guards this year to stop them, as well as the starving Ukrainians and Rumanians who regularly entered Poland, from buying all our food in bulk or simply begging for it. Yes, things have changed.'

180

As we approached the hotel I stopped to take another look at the 'Palace of Culture'. This time Malgosia smiled. 'Oh, don't worry about this lot. We wanted this kind of culture like you need fleas. Developers thought that it was too difficult to pull such a mass of concrete down so they converted it into an amusement arcade, a sports centre and a gambling casino.'

For the rest of our stay in Warsaw we tramped through the medieval town centre and many other historical relics, including the 17th century rococo style Royal Palace of the Polish Kings, all faithfully restored to their pre-war condition, although the smell of fresh paint and even paintings in some of them were obviously not what I remembered as a teenager. In the evenings we visited eating places with various standards of catering but with the help of some cherry vodka and the hospitality of my compatriots we managed to learn about this proud and long suffering nation. On more than one occasion, however, when I was pressed to reveal my part in the wartime service with the Polish Air Force, I was surprised and humbled by the expressions of the greatest respect and heroic acclaim from people, who, at the same time, had experienced nothing but deprivation and terror.

On Monday, 13th December we invited Malgosia to dinner in our hotel. We greeted her in the lounge and for the first time I realised how much she resembled my mother in the days of my childhood. She wore a home made but extremely fetching off the shoulder dress and with her deep chestnut hair flowing down in long tresses I thought I was seeing things. After a few minutes spent in mutual admiration between Malgosia and my Jynxy, who, immaculate as ever, also looked 20 years younger, we moved into the massive dining room. We sat down to a silver and flower decorated table guided by an ancient waiter, half bent with age and dressed in black who attended to the ladies with an air of elegance long lost in this modern world. In the discreet light of the crystal chandeliers one could distinguish slightly faded gold cornices at the top of tall, marble decorated columns reflecting the atmosphere of high standards and riches available to at least some people in the days gone by. Half way through our meal and at the end of the first bottle of excellent Hungarian Tokay wine, a large velvet curtain, also showing signs of old age, was drawn opposite our table. It revealed a polished parquet dance floor and a four piece band behind it. The music and rhythm of the thirties, my charming companions and the wine, would have done justice to any romantic script of an early Hollywood movie. I took Jynxy by her hand and we entered the empty dance floor to our first tango in Warsaw.

Perhaps because Malgosia explained the reason for our celebration to the waiter, and such news spreads quickly, we returned to our table to a round of applause from the adjacent tables. I looked at my smiling wife, who seemed to have experienced a sensation of being a stand-in for Ginger Rogers, and whispered in her ear, 'Darling, we have been in the wrong business all our lives.'

The following late breakfast aboard another Ilyushin bound for London was an anticlimax.

'What strange habits these Continentals have,' I teased Jynxy, 'cornflakes with vodka, my word!'

Her reply was predictable 'You didn't have to have it.'

Relaxed and feeling sleepy I looked out of the window onto an endless blue void outside thinking of the few days gone by and, for the first time, concious of my proud origin.

What would my long departed aircrew pals have given to have had this chance to return, even at this late hour, to the country they fought for and died, I thought . . . How fortunate you are, Jacek . . . born at the wrong time in the wrong place, you managed to escape from Poland with minutes to spare, lost another war in France, two operational tours in Bomber Command, ups and downs in and over the Atlantic, skirmishes from Malaya to Cyprus and your hands don't even shake . . . you don't need glasses, your hearing is good and you run like hell for a pint of beer with the Hash House Harriers . . . Maybe Jynxy is right when she says she had married a born survivor with an unfortunate surplus of energy. One day I shall tell her that some people have it and others don't and, in any case, I could not help arriving in this world on the lucky sperm of the moment . . .

Then I fell asleep.

Spruced up for the Battle of Britain celebrations in Cyprus, 1994.

APPENDIX

OFFICIAL BOMBER COMMAND
RECORDS   1939–1945

8,325 aircraft were lost

55,750 lives were lost in Bomber Command

8,195 were killed in training in Bomber Command

9,838 were P.O.Ws

125,000 served with the Command during the war

Almost a million tons of bombs were dropped

(955,044 to be exact)

23 V.C.s were won

65 pilots completed two Operational Tours

oOoOoOo